UFOs
OVER HAMPSHIRE
AND THE ISLE OF WIGHT

UFOs

OVER HAMPSHIRE
AND THE ISLE OF WIGHT

FILES OF THE UNEXPLAINED

ROBERT PRICE

HALSGROVE

First published in Great Britain in 1990 by Ensign Publications
Revised and updated 1996 and published by Halsgrove

ISBN 1 874448 10 8

CIP data for this publication is available from the British Library

HALSGROVE
Publishing, Media and Distribution

Halsgrove House
Lower Moor Way
Tiverton
Devon EX16 6SS
Tel: 01884 243242
Fax: 01884 243325

*The front cover illustrations show a crop circle;
a mysterious discoid object photographed over Hampshire;
and a hoax UFO photograph (see File 3 on 'IFOs)
which reveals how wary the researcher must be.*

Printed in England by BPC Wheatons Ltd, Exeter

CONTENTS

FOREWORD BY PAUL FULLER   7

FILE 1   THE HAMPSHIRE WAVE   9

FILE 2   A POLICE VIEWPOINT   20

FILE 3   IFOs   31

FILE 4   THE ISLE OF WIGHT ENIGMA   42

FILE 5   HAMPSHIRE'S CLOSEST ENCOUNTERS   52

FILE 6   ATMOSPHERIC ODDITIES   64

FILE 7   A PERSONAL EXPERIENCE   75

FILE 8   THE PORTSMOUTH EPISODE   81

FILE 9   VEIL OF SECRECY   88

FILE 10   THE CROPFIELD CIRCLES   99

FILE 11   THE TRUTH IS 'HERE'   109

VIEWPOINT   118

ACKNOWLEDGEMENTS   120

DEDICATION

To my favourite daughter, Sarah Jayne,
with all my love.

Note to the Reader

Whilst we have striven for accuracy throughout this project, it has not
always been possible to verify exact quotes used at the time of the various
sightings. For this, we can only apologise, and stress that every effort has
been made in pursuit of this end. The quotes used in those cases are the
author's own interpretation of the dialogue that may have taken place
under the given circumstances.

FOREWORD

For many people, Unidentified Flying Objects (UFOs) are a fool's paradise - an Aladdin's cave of fabulous treasures and fantastic events far removed from the everyday world about us. For the majority of the populace, those who have never seen a UFO, they fall into the same category as a car accident or a win on the lottery - extraordinary incidents that only happen to someone else.

This book demonstrates that people in Hampshire and the Isle of Wight, perhaps even in your town or street, are seeing and reporting the most incredible aerial objects cavorting about our night skies. *UFOs Over Hampshire* brings home to us the fact that UFOs are not someone else's problem, they are our problem and should be treated accordingly. It is important that we should seek to understand and recognize their many forms; to come to terms with the reality of their existence and open our minds to the possible implications of their presence.

Here, Bob Price has produced a fascinating collection of UFOs from the beautiful County of Hampshire. *UFOs Over Hampshire* contains a plethora of strange, often bizarre experiences, gathered from all over the County, some dating as far back as the early 1950s. Reported by people from all walks of life, they clearly illustrate that UFOs can touch the lives of everyone, irrespective of rank or title. Some of these events are well-known and have been reported extensively in UFO literature, but many more are published here for the very first time, providing valuable data for future research into the fascinating subject of Unidentified Flying Objects.

For those who are unfamiliar with the subject, some of these reports may appear to breach the bounds of credibility, bringing discredit to the phenomenon as a whole. Many others, however, are firmly planted on the borders of science itself - on the fringe of the 'natural' world, and they demand that we open our eyes to the surprises other worlds still have in store for us.

From car-stop cases to encounters with 'aliens' - from spitting balls of light to unearthly discs hovering over housing estates, the UFOs are here, demanding our attention as never before.

This books presents many UFO cases which seem to defy all the laws of logic and for Bob, as well as others, they represent one solution more than any other - extra-terrestrial visitation. It would be wrong to imply that other possibilities do not exist for the reports contained in this book, and Bob has taken pains to point this out in a chapter devoted to IFOs (Identified Flying Objects). His personal conclusion will not meet with the approval of ufologists everywhere, but none of us yet knows all the answers to the questions posed by these reports. Until such time as we can offer hard evidence for the unexplained cases, no one has the right to dismiss other possibilities out of hand. For every ufologist - and there are many of us all over the world - the excitement of the chase is in not knowing what the unexplained cases represent, and for you, the reader, there is much to learn before we can all truly comprehend the reality of the UFO phenomenon.

Paul Fuller
co-editor *New Ufologist*

FILE 1
THE HAMPSHIRE 'WAVE'

DATELINE: 24TH NOVEMBER 1954:
TIME: 0015 HOURS

It had just turned midnight, and the City of Southampton slumbered, blissfully unaware that high above their heads, a mysterious disc shaped object was silently tracking across the cold, starlit sky. It flew so silently and at such an incredible altitude - far beyond the 'ceiling' height of conventional aircraft - that it passed almost unnoticed, even to a few inhabitants engaged in nocturnal duties. One pair of eyes, however, did not miss it!

Mrs A. Marley, a member of the Southampton Astronomical Society, had braved the plummeting temperatures to study the galaxy through a fixed angle telescope from her home in Gordon Avenue. As the midnight hour passed she shivered in the bitter night air, and a feeling of fatigue began to sweep through her limbs. A hot drink and warm bed beckoned enticingly.

"Just one more quick scan," she whispered to herself, her breath hanging visibly in the freezing air. Moving away from the telescope, she took up her powerful binoculars and trained them skywards. Immediately, the object swung into view, moving due south over Southampton Water.

"I thought, at first, it was a meteorite or falling star," said Mrs Marley, who, like most astronomers, has a very practical mind. "It was a brilliant white disc, like a small moon, unlike anything I've ever seen before," she explained. Closely following the object's progress, the cold momentarily forgotten, she was not prepared for what followed...

"It stopped dead in mid-air!" the Astronomer recalled in disbelief. "I couldn't believe my eyes. Suddenly it reversed course and flew back along its line of flight." Realising that this was no meteorite, Mrs Marley kept the object firmly framed in her binoculars. "It stopped again - hovered - then took up its original, southerly, course. This time it accelerated at a tremendous rate and disappeared into space." Mrs Marley kept a lonely vigil deep into the early hours of the chill winter's morning, but the object, whatever its origin, never returned.

Over forty years have passed since Mrs Marley's sighting, and still no rational explanation has been put forward to account for it. For the County of Hampshire, they have been years of spectacular unearthly encounters, breathtaking jet fighter/ UFO interceptions, intriguing Government 'cover-ups', and terrifying 'alien' abductions! Hundreds of reported incidents have been logged carefully by dedicated ufologists, many of whom firmly believe that we are on the verge of one of the greatest events in world history - open contact with inhabitants from another planet. Incidents like the Fawley Refinery encounter...

DATELINE: 20TH MAY 1957, TIME: 0215 HOURS

Standing in lonely isolation atop one of the refinery's giant fuel tanks, engineer, Mr M. Welland took time to glance briefly at the sprawling network of pipes and buildings spread out below him. Thousands of night lights cast an eerie, enveloping glow over the huge complex - a glow that didn't seem quite to reach all the dark shadows of his towering perch. Turning back to his work he involuntarily looked up - straight at a sight that seared itself into his mind with numbing clarity.

"A black, elliptical, object was spinning across the sky at an amazing speed. It had a reddish, pulsating, centre and an orange glow around the edge". The ex-Merchant Navy navigating officer described its course. "It flew in an arc, SE to SSW at 40-45 degrees elevation."

Feeling a thrill of fear as he confronted the unknown from his exposed and vulnerable position, he backed towards the rim of the tank, calling for one of his colleagues to share the experience. More than ever before, he felt a desperate need for the presence of another human being.

"It shot overhead at a phenomenal speed, spinning like a Catherine wheel," said the shaken engineer. "By the time one of my mates arrived to find out what all the shouting was about, it had gone."

Of one thing he was quite sure. In all his years with the Merchant Navy and during his time with the R.A.F., he'd never come across anything like it before.

Sporadic sightings occurred throughout the '50s and '60s. Southampton, for some mysterious reason, seemed to be the 'chosen' city, with dozens of sighting reports flooding in. It quickly became apparent that the south's UFOs were not just figments of fevered imaginations. Engineers, Doctors, Policemen, Pilots, Teachers - men and women from all walks of life, were reporting strange aero-forms in the skies of Hampshire. Whilst a large percentage were explained away, many others remained unidentified. Why?

Although a great many 'nocturnal light' UFOs were later found to be natural phenomena (shooting stars, comets, etc.), others defied any known laws of human science and technology. They remain, to this day, unexplained.

DATELINE: 26TH OCTOBER 1967.
0430 HOURS

On a long, lonely stretch of road, just outside the village of Hook in North Hampshire, a solitary vehicle moved steadily through the stark, moonlit landscape. Company Director, Mr B. J. Colley, en route for the Midlands in his Ford Transit van, checked his watch and noted, with satisfaction, that he was well on schedule.

Twirling the dial on his cab radio, he found some early morning music to lift his spirits and settled himself comfortably for the rest of the journey.

Without warning the music stopped abruptly, the engine cut-out, and the lights failed completely. Stunned at this sudden turn of events, Mr Colley sat perfectly still in his cab, the darkness and silence closing in on him like a blanket. Recovering quickly from his surprise, he reached for the ignition key and turned it sharply.

Nothing!

Feeling slightly anxious at this unexpected delay, he climbed down from the cab and opened the bonnet of the Transit, expecting to find a loose wire to account for the stoppage. Expertly checking over the electrical system he could find no logical reason for the breakdown. Deciding to try the ignition once more, he closed the bonnet and turned towards to cab. Out of the corner of his eye he caught sight of a dark object hovering over the road ahead, casting a long shadow in his direction. Mr Colley takes up the story in his own words...

"To be honest, I was so pre-occupied with the thought of being delayed that I didn't take much notice of it and once I was back in the cab, it was too high for me to see anyway," he explained. Crossing his fingers, he turned the ignition key. The engine burst into life immediately, the lights blazed on and the music blared into his startled ears. Mystified, yet very relieved, he engaged gear and moved off. Seconds later, the same, inexplicable stoppage occurred again. By now, thoroughly alarmed at the possibility of a serious delay, Mr Colley hastily clambered down to re-check the engine.

"As soon as I was outside the van I noticed a strange pressure on my ear drums," he recalled. "Very much like the feeling you get in an aeroplane. I even tried the familiar remedy of holding my nose and blowing hard to try and clear it." But that wasn't all...

"An overpowering smell hung in the air - like an electrical dis-charge," said Mr Colley. This time, when he looked up the road, the object, which was much closer than before, held his full attention. It was now less than a hundred yards away, directly over the road in front, hovering at around fifty to a hundred feet - in absolute silence!

He later described the object as being, "curved on top, with a squat, conical undersurface." The size was approximately 60ft wide by 30ft high. The moon glinted off its dark, metallic surface.

Mr Colley was later to insist to investigators (Dr Bernard Finch and Mr R. Winder) that the object was definitely under intelligent control. Time stood still for the man on the ground as he waited, helplessly, for the unwordly craft's next move.

He caught his breath in sudden surprise as the object started moving away from the road and out across the open countryside. "It didn't turn or tilt in any way," stated Mr Colley. "There was complete silence as it simply flew across the trees, gathering speed as it went."

Alone at last, he returned to his van and found that the engine fired first time. Taking one last look around, at the scene of his encounter, Mr Colley drove off into the gathering dawn. Few people had ever experienced such an awesome confrontation.

From Portsmouth to Lymington, Andover to Basingstoke, Winchester to Gosport - the sightings continued. Some were in isolated locations, other in densely populated areas. They came in all shapes and sizes, large and small. Alone or in formations of two or more...

DATELINE: EARLY AUTUMN 1979. TIME: MIDNIGHT APPROX.

For Pete and Marilyn Smith, a pleasant evening out was drawing to a close. Pete's sister and her husband, who were acting as hosts at their home in Pound Street, Southampton, had just served up a final cup of coffee to round off the night.

"I'd just settled back in my chair, when my sister suddenly pointed out of the window," recalled Pete in a recent interview. "She'd spotted something strange in the sky and asked us to take a look".

All four crowded up to the lounge window and immediately caught sight of an unusual aero-form.

"I thought, at first, that it was just a low-flying, slow moving aeroplane from either Hamble or Eastleigh," said Pete, "but as it drew closer, I could see it was no ordinary aeroplane. It was a huge triangular shaped craft, with a sort of white glow coming from the front. It was very low - no more than a hundred feet above the flats.

The UFO, in complete silence, flew directly over the four witnesses,

Peter and Marilyn Smith show the viewpoint from where they both witnessed a giant triangular shaped UFO flying low and very slowly over pound street, Southampton (photo S. Gerrard).

displaying a combination of colours on its underside as it passed overhead. We ran from the lounge to the back bedroom as it disappeared," Marilyn told me, "it came into view almost straight away, still moving slowly. We watched until it went out of sight and then, quite clearly, we heard a low rumbling sound, like thunder, coming from the area we'd last seen it." Dashing back into the lounge, they made straight for the window, in the hope of catching another glimpse of the mysterious object.

"A large, stationary bright light hung in the air some distance away," said Pete. "A smaller second light was moving rapidly towards it from the left and seemed to merge with the larger object. Then it just shot across the sky at a terrific speed and disappeared.

In a state of high excitement, they rang Eastleigh Airport. Surely something that big would show up on a radar screen? Unfortunately, it hadn't. An airport controller also confirmed that no scheduled aircraft movement had taken place that night either. They received the same reply from Hamble.

Marilyn described her feelings at the time...

"Quite honestly, if anyone had told me they'd seen what we saw, I wouldn't have believed them. As it flew over, I wanted to run out and knock on people's doors to get them out into the street to see this fantastic machine."

She didn't, of course. Banging on doors at midnight and shouting for the neighbours to come and look at a UFO, is not an acceptable form of behaviour. In fact, it took Pete and Marilyn Smith some years to make this sighting available for publication. Belated though their report may have been, it was, nonetheless, an invaluable contri-

bution to the study of UFOs in the South of England.

The vast flatlands of the New Forest seem to act as a beacon for these unidentified visitors, and an unusual array of flying objects were frequently observed over its wide land-mass. Could it be that they were searching out a suitable landing ground? The idea seemed far-fetched, and indeed, most UFOs kept to a safe altitude, until...

DATE: 5TH NOVEMBER 1967. TIME: 2330 HOURS

November 5th, the one night of the year when sky rockets, bright lights in the sky, and brilliant aerial explosions surprise no one. This night proved no exception, but with midnight fast-approaching, the display appeared to be over for another year.

Long-distance lorry driver, Carl Farlow, from Dawley in Shropshire, was not sorry. There was danger enough in his chosen profession without the added distraction of exploding fireworks.

Driving on the western edge of the New Forest, mid-way between Fordingbridge and Ringwood, he was approaching the village of Ibsley, easing down a gear as he did so. Although, as far as he could see, he was alone on the road, he was a firm believer in the use of caution when driving through built-up areas. Glancing in his rear view mirror a few minutes later, he saw the cosy lights of the village starting to recede into the distance. Turning his attention back to the road in front, he caught sight of a bright light, high in the sky to the west.

"Not another firework," he muttered in exasperation. This one though, seemed to be taking a long time to burn out. "As it drew closer, I could see it starting to come down." Still clinging to the belief that he was watching an expensive firework, Carl again gave his full concentration to the job in hand. Headlights appeared in the distance, and for some inexplicable reason he felt glad to have the company of a fellow driver on this lonely stretch of road. "I could still see the light descending, it looked as though it might fall between my lorry and the on-coming car," he said.

Slowing down in anticipation of a possible accident, he saw the headlights of the approaching car suddenly blink out. At the same time, without warning, his own lorry shuddered to a halt.

"Just before my lights failed, seconds after the breakdown, I could clearly see the other vehicle, a Jaguar, stationary on the side of the road facing me." About to jump down and investigate, he suddenly froze, his hand still on the door handle. With a growing sensation of fear, he realised what had stopped him. "It was a dark stretch of road in the open countryside," he recalled, "but even though no lights were showing on either vehicle, the road between us was brightly lit!"

Leaning forward in his cab, Carl craned his neck upwards, looking for the source of the strange light. Still half expecting to find some form of firework dropping out of the sky, he was stunned to see a large, cigar shaped, object, descending slowly.

"It had a white dome underneath," he remembered. "I'd estimate it to have been about 12ft long, with green lights visible along its fuselage. It sank slowly towards the ground and landed gently on the road," said the shaken driver. "It could have come down anywhere, but it appeared to pick that spot very carefully." Carl made no attempt to approach the landed UFO. The driver of the Jaguar, likewise, showed no inclination to leave the safety of his car.

The two men stared mesmerised - at what? The landed object didn't appear to be occupied - yet it was definitely under some form of intelligent guidance.

"It stayed on the ground for a couple of minutes at least," estimated the lorry driver. "I just sat there, waiting for something to happen. Looking back, I suppose I could have made an effort to get a closer look, or even tried to prevent

An artist's impression of a sighting reported in America, similar to the mysterious night-time encounter witnessed by Carl Farlow on the edge of the New Forest.

it taking off again, but at the time it seemed wiser to stay in the cab!" The object stayed on the same spot for the duration of the landing. When it lifted off again, it rose slowly above the two vehicles, waiting until it was well clear before accelerating rapidly into the night sky.

Simultaneously, the headlights of both vehicles flashed on and the engine of the Jaguar burst into a throaty roar. One strange aspect of this case remained. Although the Jaguar's engine cut out completely, the engine of Carl Farlow's lorry continued to run. He could not, however, obtain any forward motion until the UFO had gone.

In a state of high excitement, Carl clambered out of his cab and ran towards the Jaguar, desperate to speak to the man behind the wheel.

"I was going to call the police," he said. "I needed another witness to confirm the sighting." Unfortunately, the driver of the Jaguar told him that he'd been drinking and wasn't prepared to wait for the police to arrive. "I pleaded with him to stay, but he was worried about losing his licence," he said, with obvious regret.

Carl Farlow did call the police, who attended promptly, but no evidence was found to corroborate his sighting. Despite this damaging lack of evidence, his honesty was never questioned. There's little doubt that, on the night of November 5th, Carl Farlow and the unknown driver of a Jaguar car experienced a genuine 'close encounter'.

Very little photographic proof exists to substantiate the thousands of UFO sighting claims that are submitted every year for evaluation. Even when the opportunity arises to capture one of these elusive aero-forms on film, the resulting photograph is usually so blurred and indistinct that it stands little or no chance of being accepted as evidence. Now and again, however, a remedy for that situation will be offered - and declined...

DATELINE: JUNE 22ND 1975. TIME: 1500 HOURS

Monty Warlock was enjoying a peaceful summer's afternoon in the back garden of his home in Hill Lane, Southampton, when the excited shouting of his neighbour's children drew his attention momentarily.

"I didn't give it a lot of thought at the time," he told me in a recent interview. "You know what kids are like when they're out playing. Then I heard Harry, my neighbour say, 'I've never seen anything like it.'"

Still unaware that something unusual was taking place, Monty carried on with his gardening.

"There were several visitors sat on Harry's balcony at the time, as there usually were during the summer months," he recalled, "and I can remember a bit of a commotion coming from that direction."

Standing up to see what all the fuss was about, he was just in time to see his neighbour leaning over the garden fence.

"He shouted for me to look up in the sky," said Monty. "When I did, I could plainly see a very bright object hovering overhead. It looked for all the world like a glass chandelier hanging in the sky."

Estimating the object's height at several thousand feet, Monty noticed what appeared to be extremely bright lights dotted around the main body, but admitted that it could easily have been the sun's rays reflecting off its shiny surface.

"It was a fantastic experience just watching that thing up there," he said. "It seemed to be pulsating slowly all the time. Harry's wife came dashing out with her camera and took several photographs of the object".

At this stage, it was felt that someone should be notified as to the object's presence, in the hope that it could be photographed with

Monty Warlock points to the position in the sky where he and several neighbours witnessed a 'hovering chandelier' UFO (photo S. Gerrard).

An unexplained UFO sighting captured by an amateur's camera over Hill Lane, Southampton - the location of Monty Warlock's sighting in 1975. The inclusion of the garden furniture as perspective in the photograph is extremely useful.

a modern camera (the one in use being a rather dated model). A phone call was quickly put through to a local newspaper, but an incredulous reporter refused to take the call seriously. Monty laughed as he remembered the heated exchanged that followed.

"Harry's wife was part French, with a fiery temper to match," he said. "She shouted down the telephone at this poor chap, 'You just get off your backside and earn the money that's paid to you." Needless to say, that didn't go down very well, and we never did get our photographer."

The object remained in the same position for almost ten minutes, then suddenly turned on end. The pulsating increased rapidly as it began climbing higher into the sky. "I've no idea what it was, or where it came from." said Monty.

POSTSCRIPT:

A copy of the photograph, given to Monty by his neighbour, shows a golden coloured, doughnut shaped object at high altitude. Despite several enlargements, there isn't enough clear detail to form an accurate opinion as to its identity. It may, of course, have been a very different story had a press photographer with a modern camera been sent to the scene. A telephoto lens could well have gone a long way to solving at least part of this UFO mystery.

It takes a certain amount of courage and self confidence to report a UFO sighting, and it's a safe bet that many witnesses remain silent through fear of ridicule.

Even though we have sent men to the moon and unmanned probes into deepest space, sceptics still cannot accept that other civilisations, should they exist, are probably engaged in similar projects. UFOs in their myriad forms, do exist. They are a global phenomena. Great Britain is high on the list of countries experiencing above average UFO activity - this wave of sightings in Hampshire helped put it near the top of that list.

Monty Warlock with author Bob Price showing off the photograph taken by his neighbour during their unexplained sighting of a UFO over Hill Lane, Southampton, in 1975 (photo S, Gerrard).

FILE 2
A POLICE VIEWPOINT

DATELINE: 17TH OCTOBER 1988.
TIME: 0217 HOURS.

A strange lull had settled over the Command Control Room at Winchester Police Headquarters. Blue shift, half-way through their tour of duty, began to relax. In the subdued lighting, tired faces were illuminated by the ghostly, green glow from their VDU screens. Nobody spoke - they all knew the respite wouldn't last long. Police control rooms are not renowned for their peace and quiet!

The harsh shrill of an incoming triple nine call shattered the silence. It was answered immediately by a dark-haired WPC, controlling the Winchester sector. "Police emergency. Can I help you?"

She paused, listening intently, while she made a slight adjustment to her headset. "You wish to report a UFO sir?". A ripple of interest spread around the room - nobody laughed. Minutes later the radio of a cruising squad car crackled into life.

"Sierra-Mike-two-three, Sierra-Mike-two-three, are you receiving, over?"

"Sierra-Mike-two-three receiving. Go ahead Control," came the reply.

"We have a report of a UFO hovering over a hill near Headbourne Worthy. Can you attend? Over."

"Certainly Control, what offence has it committed?"

Police crews, by nature, are a humourous breed. They are also very quick to respond to an emergency and, even as the joke was cracked, 'Sierra-Mike-two-three' was speeding towards the scene of the sighting. In the control room, the WPC controlling the incident spoke urgently to the duty sergeant.

"I've deployed one unit, Sarge. Do you want me to send a back-up crew?" she queried.

"Not yet," he replied, "Ask two-three for an update as soon as he arrives. We'll play it by ear from there." Minutes later an excited voice came through on the radio.

"Control, this is Sierra-Mike-two-three. We can see it! It's not moving at all." There was a long pause, then... "Wait a minute, Control, this looks familiar. We're almost opposite the object now."

The next tranmissions came through in seconds. "Hello, Control. Problem solved - your

UFO positively identified as a combine harvester with warning lights draped over it!"

A burst of laughter filled the control room as the tension was released. The worried informant was advised of the outcome and the incident closed on a cheerful note.,

This sighting, although amusingly resolved, serves to illustrate clearly the policy adopted by the Hampshire Constabulary regarding UFO 999 calls. A spokesman for the Force explains: "Responding to emergency calls concerning UFOs does not imply official acknowledgement of the existence of extraterrestrial spacecraft," I was cautiously informed. "However, treble nine calls are dealt with as a matter of urgency, irrespective of their content. If a member of the public feels sufficiently alarmed to dial 999, whether it be to report a burglary, vandalism, or a UFO, then they have a right to expect our assistance."

This right was exercised to the full on one of the most dramatic nights in the annals of the Hampshire Constabulary...

A typical scene in a police incident room during the time of prolific UFO sightings throughout Hampshire. Here Sgt George Bolton, WPC Fiona Collier and PC Bob Such decide on an official reaction to another UFO sighting in sector NG, around the Stockbridge area (photo Hants Police).

DATELINE: 18TH MARCH 1979.
TIME: MID-EVENING

The very night itself seemed to be waiting - waiting and watching! Dozens of witnesses were to recall that a strange calm seemed to settle over the countryside and a feeling of oppressive expectancy hung in the air. One described his feelings...

"It felt like the calm before a storm. I think most of us have felt it at one time or other - you just know something is about to happen and the world seems to stand still".

The calm was shattered as a huge, glowing ball of light entered Hampshire air space north of Basingstoke. It hurtled low across the night sky, ripping aside the darkness with its burning intensity. The first of over eighty 999 calls were picked up by police controllers throughout the county, making this one of the best multiple-witness sightings ever recorded.

The object, in complete silence, passed over Winchester heading south-west towards the coast. Many witnesses claimed it was slowing down and descending, giving rise to the feeling that it was under intelligent control. Others, who saw it from a distance, thought it could have been an aircraft in distress. Emergency services on the mainland and the Isle of Wight were put on stand-by in anticipation of a possible crash landing. Additionally, the crew of the police launch 'Ashburton', patrolling the calm waters of the Solent, went to immediate readiness.

Directly in the path of the oncoming aerial juggernaut, a solitary police patrol car moved slowly across Picket Plain in the New Forest.

Unaware of the events unfolding rapidly around him, PC John Forder was looking forward to the end of his shift and a few quiet, relaxing hours at home before turning in. He was enjoying the peace and tranquillity of his drive through the deserted Forest - there were precious few moments like these in the life of a busy traffic policeman. They were to be short-lived on this particular night! As he turned the car towards Lyndhurst, the UFO appeared on the skyline, brilliantly lit and very low.

"I couldn't believe my eyes," recalled PC Forder, "It was a huge, spinning globe, heading straight for me."

Growing bigger by the second, it bore down rapidly on the helpless PC. As the cold, blinding light given off by the object reached, and flooded, the interior of the patrol car, its engine cut out with a shuddering jerk.

"I jumped out of the car as it passed overhead," said John. "It

PC John Forder. His New Forest sighting led to a mass media ordeal for him and his colleagues (photo S. Gerrard)

was very low, completely silent and looked as though it might be coming down."

As he moved around the car for a better view, it appeared, inexplicably, to descend and then disappeared from view beyond the tree line. Hastily clambering back behind the wheel, he restarted the engine and headed straight for his base at Lyndhurst. On arrival he immediately filed a report.

A check with London air-traffic controllers revealed no aircraft missing or unaccounted for. Scientists at Jodrell Bank confirmed that no satellites were due to re-enter Earth's atmosphere

that night. Speculation raged for days as to the origin of this celestial visitor - that was until John Forder appeared on television to recount his experience. A leading astronomer had been brought in to give his version of the incident and accompanied John in front of the cameras. The object, he claimed, was part of a disintegrating meteorite that had been carefully tracked throughout its descent. Asked to explain the apparent silent landing in the New Forest, he stated that it was no more than an illusion. The meteorite fragment had simply flown over the horizon. He concluded the interview by saying it had, eventually, crashed into the sea. Although this was accepted as the 'official explanation', two questions remained unanswered:

1. Why were no further sightings reported after PC Forder saw it apparently 'land' in the New Forest?

2. Why did the authorities wait several days before deciding to offer an explanation on television? Were they, perhaps, alarmed at the public interest being generated by this particular sighting?

From a police operational viewpoint, the incident was closed on the night of the sighting. Controllers endorsed their 999 incident logs: 'Unidentified airborne object (possible meteorite) passed over county. No injuries, no damage.'

In accordance with force policy, the military were informed of the night's events. There was no media blackout, as suggested at the time. Every piece of available information reached local papers, radio and TV stations the same morning. Regional UFO investigators were also contacted. No attempt was made to 'gag' PC Forder and permission was readily granted for him to appear on radio and television to recount his experience. Neighbouring forces were not always so co-operative...

In 1967, officers of the Sussex Constabulary were involved in a number of UFO sightings that hit the headlines due to their apparent authenticity. In an effort to play down these sightings and to discourage further reports being submitted, a high-ranking police officer from Brighton appeared on a national television programme to 'debunk' the mystery. His men, he stated categorically, had seen nothing more than the planet Venus. Millions of viewers were left wondering how policemen, supposedly trained in the art of observation, could possibly mistake a stationary planet (bright though it sometimes appears) for a rapidly moving UFO.

DATELINE: 8TH NOVEMBER 1967. TIME: LATE EVENING

WPC Edna Wielk carefully poured a steaming cup of tea from her thermos flask and passed it to her crew mate, PC Tony Connell. It was a freezing night and they had pulled into Little Anglesey Road, Gosport, for a quick break. Gratefully cupping the mug of tea in his gloved hands, Tony Connell leant back in his seat with a sigh of contentment. Small luxuries, like a hot 'cuppa' on a cold night, were beyond value. Sitting in companionable silence, they gazed out at the night sky. A bright flare of light, directly above the submarine base at HMS *Dolphin* , captured their attention...

"We thought it was a plane at first," Edna said, "but we soon realised it was no ordinary aircraft." A vivid red and white glow shone from he aero-form as it hovered silently above them. Remembering the first rule of observation (glass distorts) they got out of the car for a clearer view.

"There was definitely something there," insisted Edna. "We had it in sight for about five minutes before it suddenly shot off and disappeared into the night." They both ruled out the possibility of conventional aircraft, helicopters or distress flares, pointing out the unusual, twin coloured, glowing light and the absence of sound. The two officers filed official reports concerning their UFO.

By a remarkable co-incidence, local MP Dr Reginald Bennett, had, that same day, raised the question of UFOs during a sitting at the House of Commons. His question was prompted by the sighting of a UFO over Lee-on-Solent the previous night by Mr Ron Kirking, a local Borough Councillor. Dr Bennett sought to find out what organisation the Ministry of Defence had for evaluating and analysing reports of flying objects not identified as aircraft. In a typically evasive reply he was told the reports were "examined only in the light of their defence implications and, so far, nothing had been found to suggest that UFOs were anything other than natural phenomena or mis-identification of man-made objects."

DATELINE: 2ND SEPTEMBER 1977. TIME: 2317 HOURS

The duty officer at Romsey police station, with a telephone pressed tightly against one ear and his free hand over the other, tried desperately to hear what the excited caller from North Baddesley was trying to say.

"Just calm down Sir," he urged, "Speak slowly and a little louder please, there's a lot of noise my end." Covering the mouth-piece he called across to one of his officers who was hurrying towards the door. "Bill. What the hell is going on? What's all the commotion outside?"

"Not sure, Skip. Some of the boys are out in the yard. They're shouting about something in the sky."

The 'something' was a circular flying object, hanging silently in the sky over the town centre. Flashes of coloured light could be seen lancing into the inky darkness surrounding it, creating an image of terrifying power. The Romsey policemen stood watching the strange craft for several minutes before it started to move off slowly towards Winchester. Quickly gaining lateral momentum, it rapidly faded from their line of vision and vanished into the night sky. They went back inside the station to report their sighting, fully expecting to be greeted with caustic comments and hoots of laughter. Instead, the duty officer quietly told them about the calls he had just taken from North Baddesley.

"I don't know what you've just seen, lads, but over a dozen witness have just reported a UFO heading our way." He paused, taking in the expectant looks directed at him. "There's nothing vague about their descriptions either. They had night glasses trained on it!" He glanced briefly down at his message pad. "They described it as a circular, metallic looking craft with red, blue and green lights shooting out of it." Looking up at his astonished officers, he could plainly see that a second description from them would not be necessary!

The Romsey UFO remains 'un-identified'. It was an incredible sighting by extremely credible witnesses and owes much of its recorded authenticity to the police officers involved.

Although this case went 'unsolved', others did not! In the wake of one of the most frightening and bizarre encounters ever recorded in Hampshire, two police officers were to prove, beyond doubt, that mysteries are there for the solving...

DATELINE: MID 1970S. TIME: LATE EVENING

In a darkened field at Langley, on the eastern edge of the New Forest, teenagers, Andrew Crouch and Elaine Thomas, eagerly unwrapped a parcel of food they had brought to feed their favourite pony.

"I can't see him, Andrew," Elaine said as she stared into the gloom. The field stretched out before her, sloping up towards a line of trees in the distance, barely visible in the darkness. As her gaze fell on the trees she noticed three stationary lights, very bright, facing down the hill towards her. They appeared to be hovering just above the tree tops.

Curiosity gave way to unease as the lights continued to stare fixedly down, as thought sensing her presence. She took an involuntary step back and clutched Andrew's arm. "Look at those lights," she whispered, "What on earth are they?" Unable to offer a logical explanation, Andrew drew her protectively closer.

"The torch, Elaine. Shine the torch up there," he said urgently.

Frantically dragging the torch from her coat pocket, Elaine directed the beam up the hill towards the mysterious lights. The beam fell far short of its target but the response it provoked from the hovering UFO was instantaneous and unexpected.

One of the outer lights tilted sharply forward and started to glide towards them, gathering speed rapidly. Recalling the episode, Andrew described the moment of terror that followed...

"It suddenly came at us at a terrific speed - straight at us, I mean, not just in our general direction," he emphasised. "It was a really frightening experience and, believe me, we didn't take long getting out of that field!" Spurred on by fear, they ran headlong through the night, tripping and stumbling in the darkness, not daring to look behind.

Andrew and Elaine's nightmare dash ended as they burst out of the clinging undergrowth on to the main road, hearts thudding with exertion and fright. They turned, fearfully, to look for the pursuing UFO, but it had vanished completely. Less than an hour later the shaken couple gave a detailed account of their unnerving experience to the local police. A general alert was broadcast but nothing unusual could be found to account for the couple's obvious terror!

The following night a police squad car, on routine patrol in the Langley area, headed slowly towards the scene of the previous night's encounter. The thoughts of the crew, PC Tony Pilliner and a special constable, were far removed from UFOs as they kept a vigilant watch on their designated beat. Deciding on a quick break, Tony eased the squad car to the side of the road, and, for the first time, noticed that they were parked alongside the very same field so hurriedly vacated by the young pair the night before. Winding his side window halfway down, he stared out over the darkened countryside.

"It looks quiet enough out here tonight, I'm pleased to say," he said to his crew mate. "Let's stretch our legs a bit and have a quick look round." The two men unstrapped their seat belts and clambered out of the car.

"Okay, Tony, I've got the torch," called the special constable, seeing his partner reaching into the back seat. They picked their way cautiously towards the fence that separated the field from the road - the torch's powerful beam guiding the way. As they reached the fence, two bright, luminous lights appeared at the far end of the field. Recalling the incident for local reporters, Tony Pillner gave his account of what followed...

"The lights were about 60ft apart - bright patches of luminosity. They started to move towards us, gathering speed. We couldn't see anything supporting the lights or hear any sound coming from them." Despite the petrifying situation they found themselves in, the two officers stood their ground as the ghostly objects bore relentlessly down on them in a seemingly, threatening manner. Tony Pilliner swung his torch up and directed the piercing beam straight at the swooping UFOs - to reveal the incredible mystery of Langley field!

"Ponies!" The word exploded from him in a release of pent-up tension. "Ponies!" he repeated incredulously to his partner as he picked out no less than five of the fleet-footed animals with his torch...

"Two of them were pale in colour and part of their bodies were reflecting a light which was about a foot across in both cases," said Tony. "We couldn't make out which part of the body the light was being reflected from, but behind us the glow from the Esso Refinery at Fawley could be clearly seen."

Both PC's stated that it had been a particularly frightening experience and could well understand the terror it had caused the previous night. A report was duly filed and the newspapers updated on the Langley 'UFO'. Thanks to the steady nerves of the two officers a small part of the web of mystery surrounding UFOs was unravelled.

THE ALTON U.F.O.

The time was 7 o'clock on a cloudless January night in 1988. Off duty policeman, Len Haffenden, out walking his dog, shivered as the winter chill seeped through his warm clothing. Len, a station duty officer based in his home town of Alton in East Hampshire, had

chosen the spacious grounds of the Lord Mayor Treloar College for his evening stroll, and had just entered the long driveway that ran along the college's western perimeter. His attention was immediately drawn to an intense white light in the sky ahead of him.

"I've never seen such a brilliant light in my life," said Len later. "It was impossible to judge its size because I'd no idea how far away it was".

The globe held position north-north-west of the college at about 60 degrees from the ground. Asked to compare the brightness with aircraft landing lights, he was emphatic in his reply. "I was brought up on the outskirts of Heathrow and the house I live in now is on the flight path from RAF Odiham, so when I tell you that light was much brighter than anything I've ever seen before, believe me, I'm not exaggerating!"

As he puzzled over the object's identity, it suddenly plummeted earthwards! "It dropped vertically until it was about 30 degrees from the ground, then stopped and hovered as before," Len observed. At this stage he decided to take a calculated risk and dash home for his binoculars in the hope of getting a clearer view of the object before it disappeared from view. In less than a minute the mystery globe sprang into magnification as Len held the lenses to his eyes.

Another unexplained UFO sighting over Southampton in April 1989. The object, seen above the bright street light, was massively large, although the effect of its size is lost amidst the 'clutter' of a bright night scene (photo S. Gerrard).

Describing the shape of the aeroform later, he likened it to a shuttlecock with a very bright light in the centre A cone of misty fluorescence trailed behind the main body. "I had problems trying to focus," recalled Len, "but I remember thinking that the tail section look unreal! It seemed as though there was something solid inside the cone of light." Both his wife and teenage son bore witness to the sighting and confirmed the description. As they continued to view the object, it suddenly took off in a westerly directions. "Faster than any conventional aeroplane that I've ever seen," said Len. It eventually disappeared into the

bank of cloud still visible on the horizon.

Len Haffenden reported his sighting to the military police at RAF Odiham and received a phone call from RAF Intelligence shortly afterwards. He was closely questioned for over half an hour by an officer who was sympathetic but very non-committal.

Like most witnesses, Len did not seek publicity from his experience - indeed, this startling and concise account of a genuine UFO encounter would have lain dormant within the confines of Military Intelligence had it not been for a remarkable coincidence. On the day following the sighting, a local newspaper reporter with an eye for a scoop, rang Alton police station for a summary of the night's events. The PC taking the call laid the phone down on the front office counter whilst he checked for any newsworthy items available for press release. At the other end of the counter, PC Len Haffenden, now back on duty, recounted his UFO sighting to an interested colleague - unaware that the reporter at the other end of the open phone line was listening intently to his every word! When the phone was picked up again he asked to speak to Len regarding the conversation he had overheard and, subsequently, an account of the Alton UFO reached an astounded public.

Police officers will continue to sight more UFOs than any other body of people because of their constant, vigilant and widespread presence throughout the country. Some will report their sightings, many others will not.

Fear of ridicule is not confined to the civilian population and, in many cases, important encounters will go undocumented because of this. The sightings that come to light will, as always, be accurate, unbiased reports from highly trained observers and will do much to sway the balance of opinion regarding the existence of UFOs.

A major survey of over 60,000 sighting reports revealed that policemen see more UFOs than any other single group of people.

FILE 3
IFOs
(IDENTIFIED FLYING OBJECTS)

'U.F.O. (also UFO). Unidentified flying object, a term often applied to supposed vehicles (flying saucers) piloted by beings from outer space.'

Dictionary definition

This popular image of UFOs has been carefully nurtured over the past few years by writers, film-makers and media reporters - the truth, of course, lies far beyond this heavily romanticized notion. Approximately 95% of all reported UFO sightings are genuine mis-identifications of natural or man-made phenomena. The other 5%, the genuine UFOs, continue to baffle everyone.

Various cult societies are convinced that they are celestial messengers from nearby planets bringing messages of hope and salvation. The 'inner earth' brigade believe they originate from within our own planet, whilst others favour the extra-dimensional theory. One school of thought has it that UFOs are based under the sea. Of one thing they are all agreed though: most of the aerial oddities reported as UFOs can be positively identified and do not merit selection for their 'further enquiries' files.

On a cold, dark winter's morning in the New Forest village of Butts Ash, postwoman Wendy Rees, received the fright of her life as a huge, glowing UFO skimmed across the tree tops towards her.

"It was just glowing up there," said Wendy, "I was absolutely terrified! It seemed to be heading straight for me." Deciding not to await developments, she leapt into her van, and, "Drove like hell back to the sorting office!" Fellow Post Office worker, Graham Bloxham, had also spotted the frightening aero-form.

"It was going at a fair old pace over the Waterside," said Graham.

The object shot past startled coastguards at Calshot and the Needles, who finally identified it as a civil hot-air balloon that had taken off from Ashton Gate near Bristol in the early hours of the morning.

Piloted by 'ufonaut' Phil Clarke of Bristol University, it was engaged on a world long-distance, record breaking attempt. This spectacular example of an IFO illustrates perfectly the effects that ordinary objects, seen in extraordinary circumstances, can have on the imagination. Thankfully, hot-air balloons usually fly by day and are low on the list of UFO mis-identifications - which should please everyone engaged on lonely duties during the hours of darkness!

If hot-air balloons are low on the list of IFOs, then stars and planets, as befits their heavenly status, are very near the top! It may seem strange that these familiar stellar bodies are so often mistaken for UFOs but statistic have proven this to be the case on countless occasions.

A badly frightened driver from Andover (anonymous at his own request) once drove at breakneck speed down a long, tree-lined road in a desperate attempt to shake off a huge, dazzling white UFO that was racing alongside him.

"I could see it through the trees," he explained. "It seemed to be streaking through the branches. One minutes it would be in front of me as I rounded a bend - the next, it would be back alongside!" It was only as he emerged from the tree cover and caught his first full glimpse of the 'UFO' that he realised he'd been trying to outpace the moon! Laughable? Maybe, but the illusion of stationary objects keeping pace with moving vehicles, particularly when seen through trees, is a familiar one with most country drivers. Stars, likewise, are frequently mistaken for UFOs. These song-inspiring cosmic objects are responsible for a high percentage of nocturnal light,

Hot air balloons often feature in mistaken sightings of UFOs. This one-man 'envelope' seen at a recent Southampton Balloon Festival does not have the familiar gondola slung underneath. These days such balloons take on all sorts of shapes and sizes - and their burners, in twilight conditions, can be seen as mystery lights hovering silently in mid air.

misinterpretations. The usual image of stars, as stationary points of white light against a dark backdrop, is far removed from the picture conjured up by erroneous witness reports.

"A revolving orb, shooting out varicoloured beams of light!" was how one skywatcher described a mystery object seen on the horizon near Portsmouth during the late seventies. Investigators were on hand when the shimmering spheroid re-appeared in exactly the same spot the following night. Immediate identification followed and the words, 'Starlight refraction' were duly logged on the report form. Refracted (or 'bent') starlight is a recognised atmospheric oddity that can produce illusions of movement and colour, especially when the stars are near the horizon.

A cluster of seven lights caused consternation when they appeared over Hythe in the New Forest. Reports flooded in and a local photographer managed to take a fairly clear picture that baffled many - but not all! The unfamiliar formation was positively identified as a group of stars known as the Pleiades.

Brighter still, when visible, are some of the planets such as Mars or Jupiter, but the king of the IFOs is undoubtedly Venus. This brilliant beacon of light has triggered literally thousands of false alarms - not to mention violent aggression...

Sailors from the American Warship USS *Houston* , who proved a great favourite with the residents of Portsmouth during a wartime visit, grimly recalled the time they responded to the heart-stopping cry of the forward lookout.

"Enemy aircraft! Dead ahead!" Within minutes the crew were at action stations as the captain heeled his ship hard over in an attempt to bring his turrets to bear. The recoil from the mighty guns sent a shudder deep into the bowels of the ship as almost 300 high-explosive shells were sent hurtling into the early morning sky. The roar of battle stopped abruptly, to be replaced by an embarrassed silence as the navigating officer politely pointed out that the 'hostile aircraft' they had been trying to blast out of the sky was, in fact, the planet Venus! In fairness to the war-weary sailors of the USS *Houston* , it should be pointed out that this eye-catching planet has been mistaken for an approaching aircraft on many occasions since!

On land too, this mischievous planet has lured mortal man to acts of incredible endurance. One excited newspaper photographer, eager for a worldwide scoop, spent over three hours driving in hot pursuit of what he thought to be a speeding UFO. Fame, and the planet, eluded him when he ran out of petrol! Not surprising when you consider that the object of his attentions held station several million miles away,

METEORS AND METEORITES

"See a shooting star and make a wish." Lovers everywhere are familiar with this romantic notion but it will probably come as a great disappointment to learn that these dream-bearing arrows are nothing more than tiny fragments of space junk burning up in the earth's atmosphere. Commonly known as meteors, they provide a spectacular pyrotechnic display for anyone lucky enough to witness their brief but glorious demise.

Most of us have seen a shooting star and are familiar with its recognised characteristics, so why then, are they also frequently mis-identified? The simple answer is that meteors do not always conform to the expected behaviour pattern widely attributed to them. A short-lived flare of downward travelling luminescence is the stereotyped image of a shooting star, yet witnesses have described them as flying in all directions - including upwards! The answer to this puzzle lies in the path (or trajectory) taken by the burning meteor.

We expect to see it zipping earthwards in a conventional arc, but what we are actually viewing is an apparent, or illusory, trajectory along our line of vision. Under these less than ideal conditions, meteors can appear to fly off in all directions and at any angle. The duration of the burn is another contributing factor to the many false reports submitted concerning meteor IFOs.

"It couldn't have been a meteor, I had it in sight for a good ten seconds before it disappeared over the horizon." Similar statements from dozens of eye-witnesses confirm the average citizen's belief that meteor burn-ups are no longer than a couple of seconds. In fact, cases of fifteen to twenty seconds duration have been recorded although this is certainly not the accepted 'norm' for meteor entries.

What are meteorites? Quite simply, they are meteors that fail to burn up completely and actually reach the earth's surface. It's our good fortune that only a minute amount of the meteoritic debris that scorches into the atmosphere by the ton survives to become meteorites!

MAN-MADE IFOs

There was nothing to suggest that the morning of January 6th, 1978, would be different from any other. Certainly not to Eastleigh rail-wayman, Peter Steward, who was working on a section of track near Southampton Road. Enjoying a brief respite from his arduous task, he chanced to look skywards and was astonished to be confronted by a huge, grey UFO. A rather shaken Mr Steward remarked later:

"It was far larger than a parachute and it looked to be even bigger than a light aircraft."

Pressed for a description he commented to enthusiastic reporters that it exhibited a dull, almost colourless hue and was entirely devoid of any type of reflection. "As far as I was concerned, it was an unidentified flying object" he stated.

The object flew inexplicably towards Eastleigh Airport and began to descend swiftly as it approached the runway. Onlookers watched it land gently just outside the airfield perimeter. Anxious officials raced to the landing site. Unauthorised craft never land without clearance, or do they?

The control tower was silent. Tense and silent. The radio suddenly crackled into life... "Unauthorised aircraft identified. Scratch one giant polythene bag!" A sigh of relief swept around the control tower and the air traffic controllers burst into fits of laughter.

There is nothing unusual about wind-blown objects in a climate like ours, where uncertain, often blustery, conditions prevail. The circumstances in which these objects are sometimes viewed, however, can quite easily promote them to phenomena status, as in the case above. Plastic bags cannot, by any stretch of the imagination, be described as a rarity. How then, could one possibly be mistaken for a UFO? The answer is straightforward. Although we expect to see them in abundance every day, we do not expect to see them soaring 300 ft in the air, flying majestically towards a busy airport!

It is a reasonable assumption, on the other hand, that aircraft are constantly seen in the vicinity of airports, but that still does not prevent numerous UFO reports being made with regard to them. Seen at odd angles or with the sun glinting off their shiny air-frames, it's not difficult to see why they are often mis-identified. An approaching aeroplane, seen head on from a distance can, quite easily, take on the appearance of a hovering, domed saucer. Simple to explain away, soon forgoten, but occasionally - very occasionally, something will appear in our skies, the like of which has never been seen before...

"I'm telling you this thing was solid nuts and bolts! It looked like a huge boomerang!" said one witness.

"I saw it flashing between a break in the clouds - a boomerang shaped object going at a phenomenal speed!" remarked another.

Sightings of aircraft such as the Stealth bomber and the swing-wing North American Rockwell B1B have given rise to numerous false UFO reports. The angle of viewing, and the flare from jet burners, especially at night, can give the impression of fast moving lights.

"Don't' try and tell me this was an aeroplane. There's not an aircraft in the sky that looks like that thing!" said a third.

These are just a few examples of the numerous reliable reports received about a mysterious boomerang-shaped UFO over the last few years.

However, investigations and speculations were cut short in 1988 by the unveiling of the B2 'Stealth' bomber, an experimental aircraft that had been flown in secrecy for a number of years prior to its inauguration. The identification of this spectacular, boomerang shaped aeroplane was greeted with

mixed emotions by UFO investigators. Genuine interest and relief at a positive identification mingled with a nagging unease as to the possibility of other secret aircraft roaming the skies. How narrow was the gap, perhaps, between a boomerang shaped craft and a saucer shaped plane with a domed cockpit? The answer sadly, lies only with military intelligence who are, understandably, tight-lipped about such matters!

Strange though the Stealth bomber may look, it certainly has not cornered the market in aerial oddities - Hampshire's own 'Bug-eyed monster' has seen to that. The 'Optica' scout, formerly used

IFO? The strange shape of aircraft such as the Optica spotter plane has given rise to a number of reported UFO sightings. This almost silent aircraft with its bug-eyed configuration is a prime candidate for an IFO.

by the police as an observation aircraft, so impressed movie moguls with its alien appearance that they cast one alongside Star Wars actor, Mark (Luke Skywalker) Hamill, in a futuristic science-fiction film 'Slipstream', Criminal offenders and errant motorists, caught by its all-seeing eye, must often have wished that the Optica confine its activities to such innocent pastimes!

AIRCRAFT LIGHTS

Night flying aircraft, displaying arrays of varicoloured lights, present a far more common dilemma to hard-pressed investigators. Often seen low in the sky, they are responsible for over 80% of all aircraft related IFOs, yet very few witnesses, when questioned, were able to give an accurate description of running-light configurations. If the need ever arose to seek a common denominator for all these cases of mistaken identity, it's a safe bet that 'absence of engine noise' would top the list. Amazingly, a number of these silent sightings were made from distances of over a mile away - far enough, you may think, to make any engine noise inaudible...

Incredible though it may seem however, many of these nocturnal-light witnesses believed the lack of sound provided sufficient grounds for ruling out aircraft activity.

Whilst accepting that the comforting roar of an aero-engine can serve to dispel many fears of the unknown, it is as well to remember that the absence of sound can be attributed to factors other than distance. Wind, for instance, can deflect sound very effectively. Combine this with the reduced noise of an aircraft on landing approach with throttled back engines, and you have the makings of a mis-identification. Add two blazing white landing lights and you have the basic ingredients for a classic UFO sighting - silence and bright light. How then, without the tell-tale whine and roar of man made engines, can an aeroplane be identified by its running lights alone?

"With great difficulty!" appears to be the answer to this leading question and, at first glance, the sentiment seems justified. As we know, aeroplanes come in a huge variety of different shapes and sizes - all bearing their own particular light configurations. Confusing enough in itself, but doubly so when myriad points of sparkling luminescence are seen from the many differing angles assumed by aircraft in flight. Navigation lights, running lights, strobe lights, anti-collision lights and landing lights, all conspire to bemuse the senses as they flicker brightly through the darkened heavens. To assist in the identification of standard aeroplane light patterns, look first to the colours displayed. Conventional aircraft will be showing three only, albeit in varying positions. Red, synonymous with danger, is the mainstay of the configuration. It adorns airframes in a variety of locations, depending on the weight category of the aircraft involved, but its one outstanding role is that of anti-collision light. Of all the spectacular sights seen emanating from night flying aeroplanes, the intense red beams sent stabbing into a shrouded night sky from these revolving orbs, must surely rank among the most awe-inspiring! Green, ghostly and eerie, the colour that conjures up the stereotyped image of a UFO. This is also the standard starboard (right-hand) wing-tip light. Look for red on the port wing, but bear in mind that you may be looking at either or both from awkward angles. White lights, blinding and mesmeric when seen head on are used as landing lights. Expect to find these in pairs or as a single unit. Familiarisation with aircraft night lights, useful thought it may be, can also have its drawbacks and it would be as well to remember that some of Hampshire's IFO sightings bore no relation whatsoever to conventional aeroplanes.

On the 4th August, 1972, a family from Lymington in the New Forest were taking in the warm night air before retiring for the night. The time was a quarter to midnight. Sanding in peaceful contemplation they took in the calm beauty of their surroundings, little realising the dramatic events that were about to unfold above them. Everything appeared to be in its place as they gazed idly around the tranquil scene until...

"Look! What's that?" Both parents moved quickly to their daughter's side and looked in the direction of her pointing finger. A pulsating, disc shaped object was clearly visible against the sky.

Mystified by the unusual aero-form, they watched in alarm as it suddenly plummeted earthwards and disappeared below the tree line, heading towards Ringwood. Minutes later the object re-appeared, further north. Training hastily gathered binoculars on the strange craft, they watched in stunned silence as it carried out numerous aerobatic manoeuvres.

"We couldn't believe our eyes at first," the family recalled. "It was a strange, saucer-shaped craft, brilliantly illuminated. It flew in all directions. The object remained in sight for approximately fifteen minutes before finally flying off into the night.

For some time this sighting appeared to be a genuine UFO encounter and caused quite a stir when it hit the headlines. Aircraft and shooting stars were ruled out as an explanation, and indeed, it looked at though the New Forest UFO would defy all attempts at identification. However, in the midst of all the excitement and speculation, the 'culprit' was unveiled.

During the night of August 4th, at precisely the same time as the Lymington family looked in their direction, the crew of a night flying rescue helicopter lowered an experimental searchlight on the end of their winch cable. The helicopter, silent and invisible due to darkness and distance, then proceeded to carry out various flight tests with the disc shaped light dangling below its darkened fuselage. The pilot, blissfully unaware of the drama he was creating, completed his trials and returned, uneventfully, to base.

Ever increasing advances in aviation technology will continue to pose problems in the field of ufology, as the Lymington IFO clearly illustrates. Rescue lights aside, there exist special mufflers to deaden helicopter noise; jump jets that can land and take off from practically anywhere; night-time in-flight refuelling (fighters often being mistaken for UFOs rejoining a mother ship) - the list goes on. Aeronautical oddities do not, thankfully, deliberately seek to deceive - a virtue shared by the majority of IFOs. But not all...

THE 'E.T.' LANDING

In the neighbouring county of Surrey, close to the Hampshire border, motorists were forced to swerve violently to avoid a gigantic, brightly lit UFO as it loomed out of the early morning mist over the M25 motorway. The squeal of hastily applied brakes echoed across the slumbering countryside as drivers screeched on to the hard shoulder, seeking safety. Local police took dozens of frantic telephone calls, all reporting the alien-looking spacecraft. Squad cars were on hand when it settled in a field rear Redhill. Approaching with a great deal of trepidation, officers were not prepared for what followed! A space suited replica of ET, (the fictional extra-terrestrial created by Stephen Spielberg), jumped from the 'UFO' to confront the ashen-faced policeman. Reeling from the shock of this dawn encounter, they received a further jolt to their nervous systems as a second figure emerged to stand alongside the first. Almost as well-known as his extra-terrestrial companion was Richard Branson, the millionaire famous for his larger than life escapades. The UFO was a cleverly disguised hot air balloon. The date? April 1st!

Branson's prank was not appreciated by everyone, but it highlighted one other facet of the UFO enigma - the hoax. Prevalent in a number of differing forms, hoaxes are acts of deliberate

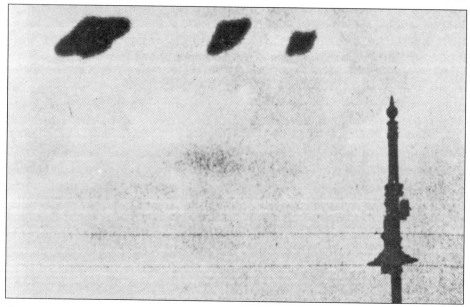

This formation of three UFOs somehwere over England was later proved to be the result of trick photography.

deception carried out for varying reasons. Very few are on the same scale as the 'ET' balloon, but they can create just as much annoyance! Some are perpetrated for fun, some for profit and publicity alone. All are a hindrance to serious investigation. On the other side of the fence are the innocent activities of responsible people totally unaware of the shock waves generated by their actions!

"A dark, barely-visible shape lit by a ghostly blue light."

"Unbelievable! It flew over in complete silence. I know it couldn't have been an aeroplane because they don't show blue lights and this was a definite blue."

"I saw it glide past our bedroom window. It was so eerie; no sound, just this blue glow". A spate of similar reports over a seven day period sent ripples of unease through the City of Southampton a few years ago.

"What now?" was the resigned question on many lips as the sightings continued. To the people of Southampton, it was a week full of UFO visitations, ghostly lights in the sky and strange aero-forms,

To the scouts of the 25th Southampton (Northam Sea Scouts) troop, oblivious to the mounting anxiety, it was no more than an experiment with a poly-thene bag, some methylated spirit and a piece of cotton wool. The bags were strengthened by inserting wire hoops around the mouth and the cotton wool, soaked in meths, hung suspended in the middle of the hoop. When ignited, the bag filled with hot air and rose to heights of 200ft. The wind did the rest. The sightings, and the experiments stopped when the two were finally linked.

IFOs do form a huge part of the UFO phenomenon, but they do not, as many would have us believe, form all of it. Nevertheless, it is important to acknowledge the existence of IFOs - to say yes, of course we are aware that not all flying objects are inexplicable. At the same time, it's important to remember that, as in gold prospecting, genuine finds do exists. It just needs a lot of careful sieving to locate one!

FILE 4
THE ISLE OF WIGHT ENIGMA

Lying off the south coast of Hampshire (11.64miles at its furthest point) the Isle of Wight comprises 146.961 square miles of land and inland waters. If you chose to run the entire length of the Island, you would cover only 22.93 miles. From top to toe the furthest points are just 13.44 miles apart. These statistics are proffered, not as a lesson in geography, but to demonstrate the fact that the Isle of Wight has probably experienced more UFO sightings than any other area of a similar size in Great Britain. The quality of these cases and the impeccable reliability of the witnesses involved are, for such a small community, exceptional.

COWES AIRPORT. 27th July 1950

Captain Jessop, ex RAF pilot, gently guided his Auster light aircraft down onto the runway at Cowes Airport and began to taxi slowly towards the nearby hangar. His passenger, George Wilks, looked contentedly out of the cockpit window at the awakening of a new summer day. His reverie ended abruptly as the pilot shouted urgently,

"Look there, George! In the sky - quickly!" Rapidly bringing the Auster to a halt, Captain Jessop, closely followed by George Wilks, jumped out for a clearer view. Both men immediately picked out a Gloster Meteor jet aircraft sweeping south at around 8,000 ft. As the aeroplane receded into the distance they became aware that it was not alone in the sky! A brilliant white light drew their attention as it flashed overhead at a height of approximately 20,000 ft - following the path taken by the Meteor jet.

"It was a hard white light, unlike anything I've ever seen before," said George. "Its speed was fantastic. I'd say it was doing at least 2,000 mph!" The engineer and the pilot watched, dumbfounded, as the oval shaped object scorched across the early morning sky.

Neither man, in all their combined years of aviation experience, could recall seeing anything of a similar nature. Although both men refused to be drawn into conjecture regarding the Cowes UFO, it should be remembered that their professions alone would have provided them with a wide experience of airborne phenomena.

That the two men did not, at any stage, forward a solution to the mystery, says a great deal for the authenticity of this spectacular daylight sighting!

It was Ryde, another Island airfield, that was to feature prominently in an unusual night sighting in the spring of 1976. The time had just turned 10.30pm when former Royal Navy serviceman, David Spicer and his wife first noticed a strange-looking bright light hanging 2,000 ft above the airport tower. As they puzzled over its identity, it made a sudden movement and rocketed upwards in a vertical climb.

"I've never seen anything move as quickly as that thing," said David. "Its rate of climb was un-believable!" At the top of the climb, the UFO hovered moment-arily before banking over and flashing back towards the startled couple.

"When it was almost overhead it stopped again and just hung in the air above us."

Describing the aero-form later, they likened it to a spherical black mass with red lights showing all around the perimeter. The astonished couple confirmed, with some conviction, that the object they had seen, although bearing no sim-ilarity to conventional aircraft, flew in a controlled manner and was, undoubtedly, a machine!

During the upsurge of UFO sightings in the late 60s to mid 70s, Island residents bore witness to several 'nuts and bolts' type incidents that reinforced the theory that many of these flying machines are solid, incredibly sophisticated (by our standards) examples of a superior technology.

An unparalleled sequence of events followed the reporting, by two schoolboys, of a 37ft wide UFO flying low over Whippingham in July 1967. Spotting the hovering object near their school at a distance of approximately 500ft they watched in amazement as it slowly gathered forward mo-mentum and skimmed low across the surrounding countryside before vanishing in the distance. Questioned by a local investigator, Len Camp, the boys pointed out where they had first seen the hovering UFO. Len, whose book *Piece for a Jigsaw* gives details of his own theory on UFO propulsion units, led his group of researchers to the scene - little realising that he was embarking on an investigation that was to last six long weeks!

The two young witnesses had made no attempt to check the area of their sighting prior to Len's involvement, and were totally unprepared for the shock in store as they approached the scene. Less than 490ft from the point at which the boys first saw the UFO, a four yard swathe of flattened barley marked the beginning of its departure route.

"The barley was pressed into a deep trough," explained Len, "A continuous whirligig pattern ran right along its whole length."

The trail of destruction ran for almost three-quarters of a mile, ending near the River Medina. Farmers could offer no logical explanation for the damage, and were totally baffled by the curious characteristics of the flattened barley. "Every couple of yards little twisted tufts of the crop would be seen with broken and bare heads," continued Len. "The ground in the centre of these tufts looked as thought all the roots, soil and stalks had been forcibly ripped out."

Civil Aviation officials were flown in to evaluate the damage but admitted to being utterly at a loss for an answer. One chilling aspect of this inexplicable case remained. During the long investigation, Len Camp had increasingly been drawn to the actual pattern of damage caused by the unknown object. His excitement mounted as realisation set in with an unnerving certainty, yet still he hesitated to voice his thoughts. In the event, it took the calm approach of one of his colleagues to bring the shattering revelation out into the open.

"It looks very much, Len, as though the physical markings left by that thing, support your own UFO propulsion theory exactly!"

Observations of unidentified flying objects, accompanied by physical evidence of their presence, are extremely rare and constitute only a tiny percentage of the vast numbers of reports submitted for evaluation. The Whippingham incident provided both cause and effect, but it was not the first case on record of unexplained damage found amidst the Isle of Wight's arable farmlands. On a bright, autumn morning in 1964, a Niton farmer discovered a large, mysterious hole gouged out of the middle of his largest field. Nonplussed by his find, the puzzled farmer checked the surroundings. There were no markings to indicate that a farm machine or any other form of intruder, man or beast, had paid a nocturnal visit to his damaged field. The gaping hole, its sides clean and sharp, went straight down for almost five feet. A sharp bend at the bottom led to another ten foot vertical drop. Of the considerable amount of soil that must have come out of such a hole, there was no sign! It was as though it had been sucked cleanly from the ground by some form of device suspended directly above the hole. Local investigators at the site put forward the theory that a UFO may have dropped low enough to collect a sample of the earth's surface, but this fanciful idea had one drawback. Unlike the Whippingham incident there was no corroborative UFO sighting reported in the vicinity of the damaged field. The mystery remained unanswered, yet a logical solution was never put forward to account for the neatly removed cylindrical mass of dirt and stones. Stealth and concealment however, were certainly not on the agenda for a formation of daylight discs seen, and heard, over Newport in September 1976.

The small proportion of residents of the Pan housing estate who were out of doors at the time of the initial sighting, were ill-prepared for the shattering intrusion that was about to turn peaceful normality into an encounter with the unknown. One witness described a low humming noise just before two silver-grey oval discs appeared directly above the estate. Time seemed to stand still for the hapless pedestrians. Among those caught in the open during the whole frightening episode was a local nurse, Shirley Rimmer. She remembered the moment when the objects sud-denly accelerated and shot off across the houses.

"The sound was incredible - like deep thunder, it was terrifying. The whole area trembled as though an earthquake had hit us!" Shirley, along with other witnesses, re-marked on a strange noise accompanying the departure of the alien craft. "Like the chiming of church bells!" she recalled. Another account came from Tim Woodward, who was indoors at the outset of the encounter. He takes up the story...

"The roar as they passed overhead shook my house so violently that I dashed outside to see what was happening."

Out in the garden, he saw a formation of at least five discs streaking towards Godshill at lightning speed. "They stopped and held station over Godshill for a few moments before shooting off out to sea," he recalled.,

These amazing flying discs, despite many endeavours, are still defying all attempts at identification in terms of currently understood phenomena.

Sightings continued at random locations over the Island during the 70s, some no more than lights in the sky attributable to various phenomena - others not so clear cut. At the beginning of August 1977, an event occurred over the Isle of Wight that gave new meaning to the term 'shooting star'. The occurrence was wit-nessed from mainland Beaulieu.

Stifling a yawn as she glanced at her watch, Mrs Barbara West decided that 11.30 was more than late enough for her to be up, let alone her thirteen year old son, Mark. Calling the time out to him, she noticed that his attention seemed to be fixed on the night sky outside their living room window. Mildly intrigued, she moved to her son's side and followed his gaze towards the Isle of Wight. Directly over the Island, due south of their position, she immediately picked out what, at first, appeared to be a very bright star. In an attempt to get a clearer look at the mystery object, Mrs West flicked off the light switch and rejoined Mark at the window. His keen young eyes spotted an abnormality first.

"There's something rotating on the surface of that thing," he whispered to his mother.

Fully awake by now, Barbara West leant forward for a clearer view. "Something small and bright, like a falling star, suddenly streaked away from the main body of the larger object and descended towards the Island," she recalled. "The same thing happened again shortly afterwards, but the brightness of the larger object never varied." Unwilling to leave their darkened vantage point, mother and son continued to view the motionless aero-form, awaiting further developments. They weren't long in coming.

"Fifteen minutes later another ball of light rocketed earthwards but this time the large light-form rose vertically, levelled out and accelerated out of sight towards Southampton."

"Why?" you may ask, "if this UFO was so prominent, were there only two witnesses?" The answer to this oft spoken question is twofold. First, think back to the last time you took a good, long, look at the sky for any length of time. The chances are that most of us spend very little of our lives studying the ever changing skyscape and,

consequently, wouldn't see anything unusual going on even if it was overhead. Sightings occur, more often than not, through pure chance - the casual glance up, an eye-catching flicker of light at the right moment or an unusual sound to draw the attention are the usual preludes to a UFO experience.

A second reason, sadly accounts for the loss of more eye-witness evidence than any other - fear of ridicule; report a UFO and it's almost inevitable that 'little green men' jibes, adverse publicity, or plain disbelief will lead to bitter regret at ever mentioning the sighting in the first place. Result? A general reluctance to become involved in the controversy despite having witnessed a scientifically important event.

On the night of 14th January 1976 an Isle of Wight couple were drawn into the web of mystery surrounding unidentified flying objects. No such reluctance, to their everlasting credit, prevented them from releasing details of what was probably one of the most authentic and awesome encounters of its kind.

It was 12.40am, when the Trinity House Pilot's assistant, Rod Riddell paused in the act of locking the back door of his house in Elmfield, Ryde. The night itself was still, cloaked in a layer of low-hanging cloud that threw a mantle of darkness over the Island.

Something, however had pierced this shield of blackness with a penetrating shaft of blinding light, and it was this celestial beacon that had attracted the man's attention as he prepared to lock up for the night.

"It appeared as a stationary point of bright light, just north of Ryde," explained Rod., "Then suddenly it seemed to grow brighter and started moving slowly towards the house. I shouted to my wife, Jennifer, to come and see what was happening."

Estimating its altitude at around 300ft, well below the cloud base, Rod and Jennifer watched in frightened anticipation as the huge object drew even closer. "We couldn't see the top of the craft where the source of the bright light was obviously situated, but the glow from this light silhouetted the object's shape perfectly," said Rod.

The UFO's silent approach (at a speed estimated at around 30mph) gave the astounded couple, ample opportunity to study its size and structure.

"I'd say it was at least 100ft long and about 50ft wide," said Rod. "There was no sound whatsoever. It was very eerie!" Describing the object's shape, he likened it to a huge hovercraft. In silent splendour the UFO passed majestically overhead, oblivious to the effect it was having on the two Islanders below.

"Frightening and incredible," commented Jennifer, shuddering as she remembered the chilling event.

"As it cleared the house, the light seemed to get brighter and it began picking up speed really quickly," she continued. "It finally accelerated at a phenomenal speed, sort of angled upwards and shot into the clouds!"

The shaken couple went back indoors to discuss their frightening experience and decided that a detailed report should be submitted at the earliest opportunity to allow a thorough investigation to be made of their strange encounter.

Early the following morning, Rod rang the duty controller at RAF Thornely Island, an air base located near the village of Emsworth on the Hampshire mainland, and recounted the happenings of the previous night.

"I thought that might be the end of the matter." said Rod, "Yet within five minutes of ringing Thorney Island, I took a call from the Ministry of Defence to say that an investigator would be arriving shortly to interview us. They seemed very interested in our sighting."

Whatever the result of the Ministry investigation, it certainly never saw the light of day. In a letter from

Whitehall, Rod and Jennifer Riddell were informed that their report was being examined only to see if it had any defence implications! In familiar official prose the letter continued, "We cannot undertake to pursue our research, other than for defence implications, to a point where a correlation with a known object is established, nor to advise you of the probably identity of the object seen."

For the Ministry of Defence to send an investigator at all, shows more than a passing interest in UFO activity and, on this occasion, a little-known fact came to light that suggested why this particular sighting was being treated with so much 'official' respect. At 12.25am, fifteen minutes before the Riddells saw the UFO, a Royal Air Force meteorological officer observed the same object manoeuvring over the Solent prior to flying off in the direction of Ryde. Unlike the Isle of Wight couple, the RAF man was fortunate enough to get a glimpse of the source of light on top of the UFO's upper deck and his observations convinced him that the domed beacon was the craft's power source, dimming as its speed decreased and glowing with pulsating brightness as it accelerated quickly away over the water. His corroboration of the Riddell's sighting gave enormous credence to the whole incident, and served to place the Ryde UFO high on the shortlist of genuine encounters with the unknown.

POSTSCRIPT:

During a telephone conversation with Rod Riddell in May 1989, I raised the question of the MOD investigation, hoping for an update of their findings. Sadly, I was to be disappointed...

"I've received nothing at all from he Ministry since getting their acknowledgement of my initial report in 1976," Rod told me. "I find that very frustrating, because the sighting was such a good one and nothing that has happened in the intervening years has persuaded me that the object we saw that night was anything other than a genuine UFO!"

Following my call to Rod Riddell, I immediately phoned the Ministry of Defence who, though courteous and polite, would only tell me that UFO reports dating back more than five years were no longer accessible.

Much has been written about government cover-ups regarding UFOs and a closer examination of this 'veil of secrecy' aspect is made in a later chapter. Suffice to say, at this juncture, that the MOD's stance on unidentified flying objects remains unchanged. "Reports will be examined in the light of possible defence implications only." It now seems likely that any conclusions reached by the MOD regarding the identity or origin of the Ryde UFO, will remain locked in the dusty vaults of Whitehall.

Similarities in the shape and the size of UFOs are frequently noticeable when studying large numbers of reports, and the Isle of Wight sightings are no exception. Compare this account from a farmer at Adgestone with the Riddells' description of the size and characteristics of the UFO seen over Ryde...

"It was about 6.30 in the morning - I was just getting the cows ready for milking," recalled farmer Tom Reynolds. The animals, he remembered, seemed unusually nervous that morning but, at the time, he didn't give it a lot of thought. As he went about his preparations, a huge, brightly lit object suddenly appeared very low over the farm buildings.

"It was no higher than 150ft and completely silent," the farmer said. "I couldn't quite make out the shape of the object but it was at least a hundred feet long and about thirty feet wide."

Tom Reynolds watched in stunned surprise as the massive UFO flew past, heading in the direction of Brading Down, "It was more than a little frightening I can tell you.":

This incident took place in 1975, one year before Rod and Jennifer Riddells' sighting. However, note the similarities of size, speed, noise level and the height of the two craft! A remarkable coincidence - or the same UFO?

Rodgerbrook Farm, Newport, provided yet another agricultural backdrop for a startling LITS (lights in the sky) encounter that took place as recently as August 1988. Witnessed by Veterinary Assistant, Jane Fries, and two friends, the sighting lasted for over ten minutes and left them in no doubt about the object's ability to fly in a controlled manner.

The gathering dusk, heralding the end of another day, cast long shadows of impending darkness over the still and peaceful acres of Rodgerbrook Farm. The fading blue of a clear sky slowly gave way to the darker hues of twilight, broken only by an emerging star or two. Another idyllic end to a busy day seemed set for the three friends as they strolled in quiet companionship around the farm that was also Jane's home. Suddenly, amidst the slowly awakening stars, high in the western sky, a vivid flash of white light flared out of the gathering gloom.

"It took on the appearance of a bright white disc that I thought was getting bigger and bigger," said Jane. "I got a terrible shock when I realised that it wasn't growing in size,but whizzing straight towards us." As it drew closer, the shape materialised into a perfect discoid, completely baffling the three onlookers. Ruling out aircraft because of the unusual shape of the object, they sought to place the

An unusual discoid object spotted over the sea off Southampton, heading in the direction of the Isle of Wight (photo S. Gerrard).

curious aero-form in the field of natural phenomena. The object's next move left their theories in shreds.

"As it approached our position, it suddenly banked sharply to the right," recalled Jane. "The amazing thing was, as it turned, two flashing red lights were exposed at the tail of the object!" Utterly perplexed by the curious craft they could only stare in wonder as it unexpectedly burst out of its flight pattern and sliced through the evening sky at a blinding speed! "It shot off north at a tremendous rate, faster than anything I've ever imagined," said an astounded Jane.

Ten years previously, almost to the day, another mysterious disc was observed for almost twenty minutes as it performed various manoeuvres over the Puckpool

area. Principal witness, Mr L. Warder of Ryde, an habitual early riser had spotted the disc-like object at 6.30am as he prepared for the start of a new day. Quickly calling his wife to share his experience, he raced into the garden for a clearer view.

"It looked at first, just like a ball of fire hanging over Puckpool," said Mr Warder. "When we brought the binoculars out though, we could see it was a perfectly rounded disc!" Keeping the binoculars firmly focused on the unidentified object, the couple watched with mounting excitment as it made successive turns to the right and left. "It eventually banked towards Bembridge and flew slowly out of sight," said Mr Warder.

From the description of the object and its aerial manoeuvres, there seems little doubt that it was under some form of precise control. Whether the object was 'manned' or under remote control, only time will tell.

At around the same period (mid to late 70s) a flurry of curious cases came to light that served to deepen the UFO mystery even further. From Calburne came this oddity:

"A ring of bright lights in the sky," was how one man, David Weeks, described the glowing UFO that passed over his home at 11.00pm on a mild May night in 1977. With his brother, Christopher and his brother's fiance, Anne Witty, he followed the object's progress across the night sky.

"It looked just like a halo of lights," Anne told reporters at the time. "It went shooting across the sky in the direction of Newport!" Verification of the object's existence came from a further sighting at Niton on the same night.

In October 1978, a classic 'flying saucer' shaped craft was seen descending slowly over the Victoria Recreation Ground at Newport by local florists, Mr and Mrs J. Gadd. Woken by the strange, urgent warning of their cat as it clawed frantically at their bedroom door, they watched in silence as the UFO slowed in its descent, levelled out and skimmed low across the rooftops before finally vanishing into the southern skies.

Yet another incident, in March 1979, brought the following curious account of a far from 'classic' shaped UFO from Lake housewife, Mrs J. Newton: "I've never seen anything like it in my life before. It was about 4.00pm and I was outside my house with my mother-in-law and ten year old son, Gary," remembered Mrs Newton. "We caught sight of this strange-looking sort of tube in the sky. I can only describe it as a white baton or a length of strip lightning."

The three watched spellbound as the UFO tilted sharply upwards from its horizontal position and assumed a vertical stance. "Then it just sort of spun back to the horizontal and shot off towards Arreton," concluded the baffled housewife.

Unidentified flying objects know no boundaries - they are a global phenomena. Now and again a sighting of exception quality will attract worldwide attention and another link will have been added to the long chain of UFO 'knowledge'. When the chain is complete and the mystery solved, at least one of those links will have been forged on the Isle of Wight!

FILE 5
HAMPSHIRE'S CLOSEST ENCOUNTERS

The events that took place on the night of November 14th, 1976, on a lonely road just outside the historic city of Winchester, have become part of UFO folklore. The witnesses' shattering revelations bordered on the very edge of reality and, some thought, went beyond the bounds of credibility. During the lengthy investigations that followed however, several facts came to light that stamped an undeniable seal of authenticity on a case known worldwide as 'The Winchester Mystery'.

Chilcomb village is located approximately four miles east of Winchester, just south of the main Alton road. It is also only a short distance from that mysteriously named expanse of land famed for the inexplicable appearance of 'mystery rings' amongst its cornfields - the Devil's Punchbowl! Geometrically perfect, the strange circles are believed by many to be the result of UFO visitations. However, UFOs and mystery rings, on the night in question, were far from the thoughts of the occupants of a Mini Clubman that had just entered the darkened stretch of road leading up to the Chilcombe turn-off. The driver, Joyce Bowles of Winchester, accompanied by family friend Ted Pratt, had set out in good time to pick up her son from Chilcombe Farm where he was visiting his girlfriend.

The time was 8.55pm when a bright orange glow flared sharply off to their left at a height they later estimated at around 800ft. Descending rapidly, the light disappeared from view seconds before Joyce turned right, down the narrow lane that led to Chilcomb village. Just a few short yards down the unlit lane, the terror began...

Joyce had eased the car down to a cautious 20 m.p.h. when, without warning, it began to vibrate with shocking violence.

"It just went mad," said Joyce, "I couldn't control it at all."

Struggling desperately with the steering wheel, she felt the car lift slightly off the ground and veer towards the wide grass verge to the right. "It was absolutely terrifying," recalled Joyce, "the engine was racing flat out - I thought it was going to shake itself to pieces!"

A split second later the car came to an abrupt halt, which the witnesses described as "like hitting an invisible barrier." Shaken and mystified by their ordeal, the couple were given no time to recover before the next shock hit them with devastating effect.

Following a frantic struggle to turn off the ignition, the engine finally spluttered to a stop. A silence, tangible in its intensity, settled over the frightened couple as they straightened up from their attempts to reach the ignition key - and came face to face with a sight that set their senses reeling...

Less than six yards away, bathed in a deep orange glow, a large oval object was hovering in uncanny silence.

"I just couldn't believe my eyes," said Joyce, "it couldn't have been more than eighteen inches off the ground. I'd say it was about 15 ft long and seemed to be riding on a cushion of vapourised steam that was jetting out from several points on the object's underside."

But that wasn't all. At the front of the object, a large curved 'window' formed a considerable part of the structure. Clearly silhouetted behind this were three humanoid figures, clad in silver coveralls. One of these figures, to the consternation of Ted and Joyce, moved away from the others and out of sight. Seconds later, the humanoid appeared out of the mist formed by the vapour jets and began walking slowly towards the hapless couple. Terrified at the escalating sequence of events,

Joyce could only watch helplessly as the silver-suited entity approached her side of the car.

"He was about six-foot tall," she estimated. "His skin was clear and white, but it was his eyes that were really frightening - they were pink, with hardly any iris showing."

Ted, meanwhile remained strangely calm and felt that the humanoid presented no real threat to their safety. Indeed, his first reaction was to attempt to communicate with the figure, but this was prevented by Joyce who was by now practically hysterical.

With slow, measured steps, the humanoid came right up to the car and peered through the driver's side-window, placing his left hand on the bodywork as he did so. Instantly, the engine burst into life and the headlights shone out at twice their usual brilliance. The figure then moved to the rear of the car, forcing a cry of fear from Joyce.

"Look out, Ted! He's going round your side!" Ted looked quickly over his shoulder, but could see no sign of the tall being. In response to Ted's assurances, Joyce ventured a glance out of the back screen and saw, with relief, that the humanoid had indeed vanished! When they turned to face forward again, the UFO had also disappeared. The whole incident had lasted, at the outside, five or six minutes.

"I asked Joyce if she wanted me to take over the driving," said Ted, "she was in a bit of a state,but not to the extent that she didn't realise that changing drivers would mean getting out of the car!" Consequently, the offer was firmly declined! Engaging gear, Joyce attempted to pull away - but without success.

"It felt as thought we were still up against the invisible barrier that stopped us in the first place," she claimed. However, a second attempt a few moments later proved successful, and they drove on to their destination without further incident.

The following morning, Joyce discovered a strange 'sunburn' rash on the right side of her face and upper shoulder, the side exposed to the humanoid's presence.

"It took a week to clear up," remembered Joyce. "I couldn't say for sure if it was caused by the figure's close proximity - it may just have been some sort of nervous reaction brought on by the experience."

Further proof, to corroborate the witnesses' testimony, came from two independent UFO sightings made on the same night. The first report came from the village of Curdridge on the eastern outskirts of Southampton. The time was 7pm, two hours before Joyce and

Ted's 'close encounter'. An intense orange glow was seen low on the horizon in a north-easterly direction, placing it roughly within the Winchester/Alresford/West Meon area. The witness, Mr P.J. Baker of Southampton, described the object as disc-shaped, very bright and hovering at somewhere between ten to fifteen degrees above the horizon. The second sighting took place at 11pm, two hours after the incident at Chilcomb.

Another Southampton man, Mr C. Privitt, reported an oval object heading east from the Winchester direction towards Petersfield.

"I was about three miles outside Winchester at the time, heading for home," he recounted. "Suddenly, coming directly towards me, I could see a brilliant orange light about a hundred feet up. It flew right over my car and disappeared towards the woods in the Petersfield direction."

The events of November 14th were, for Joyce Bowles, traumatic, shattering and terrifying. She wanted more than anything to put the whole episode behind her and let it quietly fade into oblivion. However, it was not to be...

One month later, on the night of December 30th, Joyce Bowles and Ted Pratt were to experience a second encounter with the same alien craft and its strange crew.

This time however, a closer contact than either could have dreamed possible, was established!

In a near re-enactment of the November 14th incident, Joyce and Ted were again travelling between Winchester and Chilcomb when the all-too-familiar orange glow appeared in the sky above. The time was 6.30pm.

"I can remember thinking, 'Oh no! Not again', when a penetrating whistle filled the car," recalled Joyce. "It started to vibrate like mad, but then I must have blacked out because the next thing I remember is being stood in a strange rom, being studied by the three 'ufonauts' from our previous encounter!"

For several long, tension-filled seconds, Ted and Joyce were subject to a silent appraisal from the strange trio. The Hampshire couple were now in a situation that was beyond comprehension - open contact with beings from another world! One of the figures, presumably the leader, then stepped forward and spoke in fragmented English, inviting Ted to examine various features of the craft's interior. He was shown a revolving central column that he took to be a part of the main propulsion unit.

"The air around the column was appreciably warmer than anywhere else in the craft," explained Ted.

Pointing to a large wall-chart displaying a profusion of navigational lines and circles, the leader then spoke words similar to, "Here is our field." Of his exact meaning, however, Ted was unsure. The alien's next words sought to reassure.

"We are not hostile to you or your people, you must believe this." Joyce's response was immediate and to the point.

"That's what Hitler said," she blurted. Aware that her outburst, with its bizarre comparison, may have overstepped the mark, Joyce waited anxiously for any sign of reaction from the alien leader. His only response to the remark though, came in the form of a gentle, verbal rebuff.

"You have a very strong tongue," he told a slightly chastened Joyce. Relieved that a potential crisis had been averted, she listened in silence as the leader again spoke at length to Ted.

"I had a little difficulty understanding all he told me," admitted Ted, "but it became clear that they intended to return at a later date and that our car had been 'marked' in some way!"

As this final message ended, the entity moved away from the two humans. Seconds later a blinding rush of white light shot from one end of the craft to the other and the two witnesses again lost consciousness.

"When we came round, we were back in the mini," said Joyce, "but neither of us could recognise the area we were in".

They were, in fact, parked near a river on the far side of Winchester - miles away from the spot at which the abduction had taken place. The whole episode had lasted little more than an hour.

Three months later, on the 7th March, 1977, whilst driving a female companion (Ann Strickland of Southampton) to visit friends in Nether Wallop, Joyce Bowles received a third visitation from the alien emissaries - this time in broad daylight.

The two friends were chatting happily, enjoying their morning trip out when, this time without warning, the car engine suddenly spluttered and died. Annoyed at the delay, Joyce quickly jumped out of the mini to check under the bonnet. The time was 10 am.

A brief flash of light caught her eye as she moved towards the front of the car and glancing up, her startled gaze fell on a bright oval object that stood silently at the side of the road ahead. With a feeling of deep foreboding, Joyce stared intently at the stationary UFO, knowing that a third contact with the aliens was now imminent.

From beside the landed UFO a silver-suited figure suddenly emerged and walked directly up to Joyce, In marked contrast to her previous experiences however, she felt no fear in the alien's presence.

Ann Strickland meanwhile, could only watch helplessly as the humanoid took hold of Joyce's hands and began to speak. Unfortunately being out of earshot, she could not hear any of the spoken communication.

Several minutes passed before the entity released his hold on Joyce and returned to the UFO. With a low whistling hum, it rose slowly into the air and flew off rapidly, hugging the ground as it gathered speed.

Throughout the months that followed the first and second encounters, Joyce Bowles and Ted Pratt endured a horde of media reporters and UFO investigators, all intent on recording every last detail. Both were subjected to intense interrogation and did not hesitate to relate every aspect of their abduction in a friendly and open manner.

Many were convinced that they had experienced a real and frightening confrontation with the unknown - others wrote it off as a flight of fancy. One investigator found the whole concept of alien abduction so unacceptable that he gave up UFO investigations altogether!

As previously mentioned, the Winchester case stretched the bounds of credibility almost to breaking point. It was unique at the time amongst the hundreds of other sightings recorded in Britain during the 'great wave' of the mid-seventies. To this day it still retains one element of mystery that awaits unveiling.

During her third encounter with the aliens, Joyce Bowles received a message that she has flatly and consistently refused to reveal. Her reply to the oft-repeated requests for more information never varies.

"When the time is right...!"

THE ALDERSHOT ABDUCTION

On the 12th August, 1983, some seven years after the astounding events at Winchester, a second abduction took place beside the Basingstoke canal in Aldershot.

The subject, seventy-eight year old Alfred Burtoo, gave such a convincing and lucid account of his experience that investigators considered his testimony to be totally reliable and regarded the encounter as absolutely genuine.

The night, as far as Alfred Burtoo was concerned, was made for fishing. Even at midnight, as he set off from his Aldershot home, the warmth of a long summer lingered in the clear night air. With his dog following obediently at his heels, he arrived at his chosen spot on the Basingstoke canal bank and set up camp prior to casting his bait.

At around 1am, Alfred poured himself a cup of tea and stood up to ease his aching limbs. A sharp stab of bright light in the southern sky caught his attention and, as he looked closer, it became apparent that, whatever it was, it was heading in his direction.

"It flew very low over the railway line," he recalled, "then it appeared to come down behind the trees near the canal towpath."

Puzzled, but not unduly worried by the mysterious light, he returned to his fishing. The growling of his dog heralded the next stage of Alfred Burtoo's close encounter.

"As I turned to find out what all the growling was about, I saw two figures in green overalls coming towards me along the towpath," he claimed. "They were only about four feet tall and wore helmets with smoked visors that covered their features."

The figures approached to within six feet of his position before stopping. Several long seconds passed before they eventually beckoned for him to follow them - which he did without hesitation.

"I was curious," explained Alfred, "They showed no sign of hostility and, at seventy-eight, what had I to lose?"

The two small humanoids led him to a darkened stretch of the towpath where a large oval object sat overhanging the water. Estimating its size at around 40 to 50 ft he noticed a set of steps leading up into the craft's interior. At a signal from one of the figures, he mounted the steps and found himself standing in an octagonal room that housed a central 'shaft'. Beside the shaft stood two other humanoids!

"I must have stood there for all of ten minutes," said Alfred. "when a voice suddenly told me to stand under an amber light that was fixed to the cabin wall."

Complying with the instructions, he moved across the room and stood under the light. The same voice spoke again, querying his age. Surprised, but still co-operative, Alfred replied that he was seventy-eight. A long pause followed this exchange before the voice broke in again.

"You may go. You are too old and infirm for our purpose." Although deeply curious about the origin of the craft and its occupants, he felt that it would not be in his best interest to risk asking questions. He simply left the craft as he had entered it and started walking back to the spot where he had left his dog and fishing tackle.

As he arrived at the site, a low humming noise prompted him to look back in the direction of the landed object.

"It was rising slowly above the canal, glowing brightly in the darkness, recalled Alfred.

The object suddenly accelerated and disappeared into the western sky. Alfred Burtoo's abduction encounter was over.

POSTSCRIPT:

Alfred Burtoo died in 1986 at the age of eighty. Those who knew him well spoke of a down-to-earth, practical man with little time for hoaxes. He was an ex-soldier, which probably accounts for his calm acceptance of the frightening situation he found himself in, and his obvious sincerity so impressed investigators that they forwarded a report of the incident to the Ministry of Defence for evaluation. The close proximity of military establishments to the sighting area, they felt, would surely move officials to at least investigate the possibility of an advance flying machine operating within the confines of MOD property. The Ministry's reply, though disappointing, was not entirely unexpected. They did not feel that any threat had been posed to the country's defence and, as such, would not be taking the matter any further.

We can only wonder at the blinkered view taken by the Government over cases like the

Aldershot incident and ponder on one final mystery. Had Alfred Burtoo not been 'too old and infirm' for the aliens' purpose, and had he perhaps been a serving British soldier from the nearby army barracks, would the government's attitude have been any different?

THE NEAR-LANDING AT HORTON HEATH

The picturesque village of Horton Heath lies in open countryside midway between the eastern edge of Southampton and Bishops Waltham. The events that took place there on the night of November 15th, 1981, took a Hampshire housewife, Jan Burnell, to the very brink of this dimension.

Jan had more than eight years' experience as a police controller to call on to reinforce her claim that she is a practical woman, not easily frightened and definitely not given to flights of fancy. It was this attribute that lent enormous strength to her testimony and prompted the following response from investigator Tony Jones, of the Wessex Association for the Study of Unexplained Phenomena.

"This sighting is as good and genuine as anything we've ever investigated," he claimed.

On the night of the sighting, Jan Burnell had just finished speaking to her mother on the telephone and was looking idly out over her back garden fence at the darkened fields beyond. As she casually glanced up at the sky, two very bright lights, one red, one white, flew into her line of vision.

"They were about 40 ft apart," guessed Jan, "they kept flashing on and off continuously and gave off a tremendous aura,"

The lights descended rapidly until they were directly over the open stretch of land bordering Jan's property - less than 300 ft away from the startled witness. They now appeared to be wider apart than at first and seemed to mark the outer extremities of a very large flying object.

"It hovered silently for a while," said Jan, "I had the distinct and very eerie impression that it was looking for somewhere to land!"

A small, piercing beam of white light suddenly shot out from the object's centre section, hit the ground like lightening and bounced back up again. With a gasp of fright, Jan took an involuntary step backwards, knocking the telephone off the table as she did so. The same laser-like beam lanced out once again, probing the ground for - what?

Seemingly satisfied with its findings, the object then rose swiftly and silently into the night sky and vanished into the

Jan Burnell at the scene of her close encounter at Horton Heath, Fair Oak in 1981, As a result of the intense media attention which followed her apparent authentic encounter, Mrs Burnell refused to comment further on the events she witnessed.

blackness. A very frightened Jan Burnell, alone in a house that no longer seemed to offer the same measure of safety and security as it had ten minutes previously, could only stare in stunned disbelief at the object's point of departure.

There has never been a logical explanation put forward for the Horton Heath UFO. It remains one of Hampshire's greatest aerial mysteries and has placed Jan Burnell, reluctantly, amongst the small but growing band of 'close encounter' witnesses who are afforded a brief glimpse of worlds beyond.

Jan herself, although seriously affected by the sighting at the time, would not speculate on the UFO's origin. To her credit, she aired her views simply and with complete conviction.

"I am convinced that it was something from somewhere we on Earth know nothing about!"

THE HEALER'S STORY

The following account of one man's experience in the aftermath of a UFO encounter is both thought-provoking and deeply mystifying. The far-reaching effects of his brush with the unknown continue to this day in a field that is every bit as controversial as the UFO phenomenon itself. The field of faith-healing.

Ernie Sears, at the time of his sighting in 1978, was no stranger to the vagaries of UFO activity. His interest in the subject was thrust at him on a cold morning in 1960 (see File 9 - Veil of Secrecy) and his subsequent involvement included a spell as Southern Area Representative for BUFORA (British UFO Research Association). All his accumulated knowledge and experience, however, did little to prepare him for the devastating turn of events that were about to change his life forever.

The beauty of a cloudless, starlit night had lured Ernie out of doors on a winter's evening in 1978. From his home in Portiswood, Southampton, he enjoyed an almost unbroken view of the night sky.

As he expertly identified the various constellations that formed an umbrella above him, he noticed a large, dark mass moving slowly across the sky in a southerly direction.

"It was extremely large," recalled Ernie, "I could see several lights around its fuselage as it drew closer. It was clearly going to pass directly overhead."

Amazed at the sheer size of the object, he looked frantically around to see if any of his neighbours were about to corroborate his sighting - without success.

The huge shape, in complete silence, passed slowly over the rooftops as Ernie stared upwards in open-mouthed wonder.

"It appeared to be a solid, metallic craft," he claimed, "I could even make out what looked like huge rivets on its underside."

With his practical, investigative mind ticking off every noteworthy aspect of the giant UFO, Ernie was suddenly jolted by a blinding flash of insight that set his senses reeling.

"It was a totally unexpected vision of stars and planets stretching away into infinity," he recollected. "It seemed as though I'd been given a fleeting glimpse of the whole universe. I could see all our own planets leading off down a long tunnel, at the end of which I could see a bright light."

The effect was momentary and passed with the departure of the UFO. Completely nonplussed at the magnitude of his experience, Ernie could only wonder at the illusory vision brought on by his encounter with the UFO.

A question mark may have hung over Ernie's 'cosmic vision', but the reality of the UFO was never in doubt. A second, corroborative sighting by a couple in the New

Forest village of Langley saw to that.

For weeks afterwards, the image of his vision remained deeply etched in Ernie's mind, puzzling him as to its possible significance. He had never been a particularly religious man and laughed at the idea that he may have had a psychic experience.

"There was nothing ghostly or unreal about that UFO," he stated emphatically. "It was a solid nuts and bolts machine and nobody will convince me otherwise. I firmly believe it was extraterrestrial, under intelligent control, and powered by a propulsion unit far in advance of anything known to us."

Several weeks passed, during which time Ernie had relegated the sighting to his record books and sought, unsuccessfully, to push memories of his vision to the back of his mind. It took an act of kindness to a friend to rekindle these memories, on a day that was to lead Ernie Sears down a new path in life - a path that he still follows to this day.

"I'd taken a friend of mine to a faith-healer he was receiving treatment from," recalled Ernie, "I had no particular feelings about faith-healing at the time, but gladly accepted the offer to sit-in on the session,"

Ernie was shown to an armchair where he watched with interest as the female faith-healer went about her business.

"I don't quite know what happened next," he admitted, "but I went out like a light. I can remember looking upwards and seeing a group of indistinct figures, all of whom seemed to be talking at once. I couldn't understand a word they were saying to me."

When he came round he found a gentle hand on his shoulder and the smiling face of the faith-healer looking down at him

"You were really away there, weren't you," she laughed.

"I explained what had happened," said Ernie, " and she just looked at me quietly for a while. I'll never forget her next words."

"Oh! Dear. It looks very much as though you're about to join us, doesn't it?" she replied.

"I took it that she meant I was about to become a faith-healer myself and, to be honest, I was more than a little perturbed. I told her I didn't think I was quite ready to accept something like that."

Fully understanding his reluctance, the healer explained that he would not be expected to enter this specialist field until he was ready to do so. That he has now been a practising faith-healer for almost ten years is ample proof that it didn't take long for Ernie to accept and answer this unique calling.

In a recent interview with Ernie, I ventured to suggest that his sighting may have been more of a psychic manifestation than a physical one, bearing in mind his subsequent induction into the spiritual world of faith-healing. His reply was emphatic.

"No. Definitely not. The two events may have been linked but I don't think so. The UFO was a very real flying machine - the healing experience was a different kettle of fish altogether."

This incredible double event in the life of one man may well seem like the product of an over-active imagination and, indeed, Ernie would be the first to agree that this would not be an unreasonable assumption. He is, quite simply, a man totally without malice who will gladly tell you of his experiences whilst neither expecting nor demanding that you believe them.

It is not the purpose of this book to explore the field of faith-healing, fascinating though it may be. The subject is included in this chapter simply to illustrate a possible link with the UFO phenomenon.

Ernie remains open-minded about such a link.

"It's possible, I don't' know," he reiterated, "as far as I'm concerned, I've been given a gift and I don't intend to waste it."

In the county of Hampshire today there are many who would gladly step forward and attest to the fact that Ernie Sears did not waste that precious gift!

FILE 6
ATMOSPHERIC ODDITIES

"On the night of the Great Storm in 1987, I saw a huge UFO break through the clouds. Flashes of lightning were flying from it - I think it may even have caused the storm!"

This starling account of a spectacular UFO sighting over Southampton came in the wake of one of the most destructive nights in British meteorological history and, although the sighting went uncorroborated, it serves to introduce a different type of UFO experience - the climatic encounter.

Another such incident, in 1954, led to a miraculous escape for Hampshire Headteacher, Lesley Handford, who considered herself extremely lucky not to have suffered serious injury during the course of her frightening en- counter.

Although no more than a schoolgirl herself at the time, Lesley still remembers every vivid detail as though it were yesterday...

The oppressive humidity in her Aunt's kitchen, for instance, and the menacing rumble of an approaching thunderstorm, are forever etched in her memory as the prelude to a shattering and dangerous brush with the un- known!

With both feet propped inelegantly on the cross-bar of a kitchen chair, Lesley sat facing the back door - opened wide by her Aunt as a measure of relief against the sultry heat. Watching the jagged forks of lightning as they picked their way ever closer, she stole a quick glance at her Aunt, who was busy preparing tea. Marvelling at her apparent unconcern for the impending storm, Lesley felt reassured by the cosy normality of the domestic scene. Even the family cat appeared unworried, as it sprawled, fast asleep, nearby.

The storm, when it arrived, stunned Lesley with its ferocity. Bolt after bolt of lightening lashed out of the clouds, followed by deafening cracks of thunder that seemed to shake the whole house.

In sudden fright, she made to untangle her legs in order to make an undignified dash for the safety of the front room. As she leant forward her gaze fell, involuntarily, on the open doorway. With a gasp of fear, she froze in the act of moving her feet from the chair's cross-bar - a reaction that may have saved her life!

Shooting over the lip of the doorway, barely above floor level, a solid ball of brilliant white light was hurtling straight at her! With almost uncanny accuracy, the light ball shot straight under Lesley's chair, cannoned into the far skirting board and flashed out into the teeth of the storm!

In total shock, she could only stare in disbelief at the spot where she had seen the object disappear. Scared and mystified though she was, Lesley began to realise that she had had a very lucky escape. Had it not been for the fact that her feet were tucked up off the floor, the object, whatever its origin, would have caught her fair and square on the legs!

Describing the incident to me in a recent interview, Lesley recalled the moment she first caught sight of the object.

"I couldn't believe my eyes at first. It was about the size of a football and moving at a hell of a speed. The poor old cat went straight up in the air with all her hair absolutely vertical!"

Convinced that the spooky object had flown out of the heart of the storm to seek her out, she ran to her Aunt in tears. "I don't think she had a clue what it was herself," said Lesley, "but she calmed me down by saying that it was only a fireball, as though it were the most natural thing in the world".

During the years following Lesley's near fatal encounter with the mysterious intruder, several reports of a similar object began to appear in the newspapers. Compare this account of a mystery light ball seen over Southampton in 1988...

On the night in question, Riverside Park, a popular recreational area on the eastern side of Southampton, lay almost deserted - its pitches and tree-lined walkways cloaked in darkness. It was early January, 1988.

By a park bench on the edge of the football pitch, three teenagers lingered for a final chat before going home. Fourteen-year-old Geoff McWilliams takes up the story...

"We were just stood around the bench, talking, when this ball of green light shot out from a gap in the trees on the far side of the park."

Geoff's two friends, Matthew Cadden and Simon Cade were quick to spot the strange sphere as it began a peculiar manoeuvre.

"It started to fly in a triangular pattern, about thirty feet in the air," said Geoff, "It looked about the size of a football".

The three boys watched with interest as the object continued to perform its aerobatics with methodical deliberation. Surprised interest, however, turned to sudden alarm as the mystery sphere made its next move. "It stopped in mid-

Geoff McWilliams and Matthew Cadden point to the spot where they first saw the UFO in their encounter at Riverside Park, Southampton.

air and suddenly veered towards us," Geoff said, "It came straight across the football pitch, heading right for us!"

Wisely deciding that discretion was the better part of valour, the three youngsters beat a hasty retreat, stopping only when they thought it was safe. Still on the same perimeter track that the park bench stood on, they turned, breathless, to look for any sign of pursuit.

"It had just about reached the bench by then," said Geoff, "As it drew level with the path, it stopped, hovered, and then started moving towards us again. It was

really scary and this time we didn't stop running until we reached my house."

Although both these amazing encounters appeared totally inexplicable at the time, an explanation did present itself, in the form of one of nature's more volatile emissaries.

The similarities in size, appearance and behaviour patterns of the two objects pointed to the phenomena known in meteorological circles, as, 'ball lightning'.

There is no clear definition of ball lightning. It remains a mystery to science purely because there is insufficient data to state categorically that it is created and formed in a proven manner. The one definite characteristic is that it only occurs (as far as it currently known) during a thunder storm.

Varying from golf ball to football size, the fireballs have a variety of colours, but are usually white. Capable of performing fantastic aerial manoeuvres, they often mislead witnesses into believing that they are under some form of control. The truth, of course, is that they are completely out of control!

Speeds also vary. Some appear to float gently like drifting balloons, whilst others have been seen scorching through the air at speeds exceeding 50 mph.

Lesley Handford's narrow escape is even more remarkable when one considers that fireballs are also very unstable, often exploding with considerable violence!

It seemed a simple enough task to lump the two sightings together under the heading of 'ball lightning' and wrap both cases up in a neat little package marked, 'Solved'. One final mystery, however, awaited an unveiling.

During the course of my investigation into the Riverside Park sighting, I asked Geoff McWilliams how far away the thunderstorm had been at the time of the fireball's first appearance.

"Thunderstorm?" he replied in puzzlement, "There was no thunderstorm. It wasn't even raining that night!"

THE 'DOUGHNUT' RING

The witnesses in this next case wrote to me following a national newspaper article on my interest in UFOs. I make no apology for reprinting the letter in full, as it contains an exceptional account of a weather related UFO sighting.

Dear Mr Price,

After reading of your interest in UFOs, I thought you might like to hear of our experience on 1st September 1982,

At 9.30am, I heard my twelve year old daughter calling me from outside to come and see something strange in the sky. It was a very cloudy day with rain due any minute. The clouds were very low down and extremely dense, but the 'Thing' was clearly visible below them. It looked just like a Polo-Mint or discus, with either a hole or depression in the centre. It was very dark grey or black in colour, but not shiny.

It travelled across the sky in an E.N.E. direction at a constant, not fantastic, speed, laying flat for most of the time we had it in view. Occasionally though, it would flip over to present a side and plan view.

My husband, meanwhile, had joined us and we looked for any sign of it being towed by anything. We even managed to focus our binoculars on it and there were definitely no wings or appendages attached to it, and no signs of a propulsion unit either. The object flew in complete silence.

I feel that I must add that we have never seen anything strange in the sky before or since, and both my husband and I had regarded reports of UFOs with more than a little suspicion. We inclined to the belief that they were made by cranks, hoaxers, people in need of glasses, or attention seekers. We are definitely none of these, so please do not print our names,

Whilst being unable to find a logical explanation for our sighting, we still feel that there must be one somewhere.

Yours etc....

There were several questions I felt needed asking about this sighting and, in July 1989 I spoke to the witness with a view to clearing up one or two points. My first concern was to ascertain the size of the object, as this had not been mentioned in the original letter.

Unfortunately, both mother and daughter found difficulty in judging the object's dimensions and, sadly, the husband died some years ago.

"At a rough guess, I'd say it was about twice the size of an inflatable dinghy, but I've really no idea," the witness told me.

The thought of a wind-blown object, such as a tyre inner tube, had crossed my mind and it was this that I mentioned next. The reply was cautious, edged with some doubt.

"It's possible, I suppose, but it certainly didn't looked as though it was being tossed about in the wind. It looked solid and seemed to be on a predetermined course. The speed never varied and when it flipped over it looked to be a deliberate act, not the haphazard actions of a wind-tossed object."

It became obvious during our conversation that the family had made every effort to place the object as some form of natural or man-made phenomena. That they failed to do so lends considerable weight to this sighting as a genuine UFO. However, sceptics, may argue that it was brought about by clouds.

Clouds, thankfully, do not feature prominently amongst UFO mis-identifications. I say thankfully, because, it if were otherwise, there'd be little time left for any other form of investigation. This is not to say that all clouds are easily

These photographs show the variety of forms adopted by lenticular cloud formations. Such unusual yet quite well-defined formations can, under certain light conditions, be transformed into seemingly solid aero-forms, thus giving rise to mis-identified UFO sightings.

identified and there are certainly cases on record of witnesses mistaking unusual cloud formations for UFOs.

Lenticular clouds, for instance, are a spectacular example of meteorological magic and have, in addition to their fantastic, shapes, one other oddity to bemuse the senses. They are apt to remain absolutely stationary.

In order to understand this phenomena, it is necessary to look at the way in which these clouds are formed, without, hopefully, getting bogged down in Met. Office jargon.

In its simplest form, lenticular (or mountain wave) clouds are formed under circumstances when strong horizontal winds hit a mountain range. The wind is deflected upward by the mountains and then flows down the other side (hence, 'wave'), When the required conditions prevail, clouds are formed on the ridge of these 'waves' and remain static because the wave itself is stationary.

Even sceptics would be hard pushed to blame lenticular clouds for any of Hampshire's UFOs though. Mountains are rare in this pleasant, but flat, southern county!

SILVER DISCS AND UFO 'NESTS'

1989 proved to be a real scorcher, with summer temperatures rocketing into the 90s, but it was the long hot summer of 1957 that produced this extraordinary account of three 'silver disc' UFO's spotted over Southampton.

Mr and Mrs D. Bolton of Derby Road, Eastleigh, were enjoying the warmth of a sunny July day, their thoughts far removed from the pressure of everyday life in a bustling city. Even Eastleigh Airport seemed to take a breather, with little air traffic to be seen anywhere.

It was towards the airfield that the Bolton's were idly gazing when a bright, disc-shaped object suddenly rose from the ground within the airport's perimeter fence and climbed rapidly into the air. Close on its heels came two more, both with the sun glinting off their silvery surfaces.

The Bolton's watched in stunned surprise as the three discs banked in formation and flew directly overhead. A high pitched whining noise could be clearly heard as the objects disappeared into the distance.

Airport officials were baffled by the sighting - nothing had been picked up on radar and none of their staff had seen the UFOs taking off. The mystery deepened as other reports began to filter through. They had definitely been seen rising above the airfield, so they must have been very close to ground level - or even landed.

Eastleigh Airport control tower. It was here that three silver discs were observed to rise from within the airfield perimeter giving rise to a rash of UFO sightings in the area.

Some people suggested that a UFO 'nest' existed somewhere in the vicinity and in this, they were proved exactly right.

The day after their sighting, the Bolton's uncovered the true identity of the three 'flying saucers' as they, along with everyone else in the district found themselves dealing with a plague of flying ants!

With the sun glinting off their silvery wings as they rose in swarms from the ground, they resembled the perfect 'silver disc' type of UFO favoured by screen-writers everywhere. The whining noise heard by the witnesses came from the beating of a billion tiny wings.

This unusual incident, brought about by the the sun's rays reflecting off a swarm of flying ants, serves to reinforce the old adage that, 'seeing is not always believing,' and introduces yet another type of UFO misinterpretation - the optical illusion.

MIRAGES AND TEMPERATURE INVERSIONS

Light rays from the sun are frequently interrupted on their journey to Earth by ice crystals and raindrops that form in the atmosphere during certain climatic conditions. The resulting distortion of these light beams can produce various phenomena that most of us are familiar with, such as rainbows and haloes. On the other hand, they can also produce something that we in this country are not so familiar with - mirages.

The image of a thirst-maddened victim of the desert, struggling towards a wavering, water-filled oasis that does not exist, usually springs to mind when mirages are mentioned, and it's a safe bet that nearly everyone can remember a particularly hot day when shimmering waves of heat seem to reflect off pools of non-existent water.

There are two types of mirage: an inferior (lower) mirage and a superior (upper) mirage. It's the second of the two that tend to fool witnesses into believing they are seeing a UFO.

By way of explanation, it's necessary to look again at light rays. They are usually bent (refracted) in the atmosphere so that the colder air is on the inside of the bend and the warmer air on the outside. Under normal conditions the air temperature will drop with altitude and, when the light rays are reflected off an object in the distance, they will 'bend'. This leads to the illusion that the object is actually lower than it really is.

Alternatively, if the temperature rises with altitude, a temperature inversion occurs. The light rays

reflected off the same object are then bent in the opposite direction and it will appear to be considerably higher than it actually is, giving rise, occasionally, to hovering UFO sightings.

ST ELMO'S FIRE

Seafarers will need no introduction to this ghostly phenomenon, yet it took a very short letter, printed in the readers' sections of a local newspaper to enlighten me as to its possible UFO connections.

My knowledge of the condition was very basic. I knew, for instance, that it sometimes appeared on ship's masts and resembled a form of ghostly lightning. I have always associated its appearance with old time sailing ships, though if you had asked me why at the time, I doubt you would be given a sensible answer.

What I did not know was that this luminous phosphorescence, formed during certain climatic conditions, can detach itself from whatever extremity it happens to be on, and fly off, en-masse, into the upper atmosphere. Just how many UFOs witnessed at sea can be attributed to St Elmo's Fire is anybody's guess!

THE U.S.A. CONNECTION

It may seem highly improbable that a UFO seen high over a military air base in America, and a low level encounter on the Winchester by-pass, could in any way be connected. But they were and dangerously so!

JANUARY 7TH 1948 - GODMAN AIR FORCE BASE, KENTUCKY, U.S.A.

Responding to an urgent message from the Godman air traffic control tower, a flight of P51 Mustang fighters, led by Captain Thomas Mantell, vectored in on a huge, glowing UFO that had appeared suddenly over the base at a very high altitude.

At 15,000 ft, Captain Mantell ordered his flight to abandon the chase as they were not equipped with oxygen. He then informed the tower that he would carry on alone to 25,000 ft, the estimated height of the UFO, in an attempt to get close enough for a visual inspection.

His next message was short - it was also the last he would ever make....

"I'm close now. It's metallic and very big. I"m going up for a good look,"

The remains of Captain Mantell and his P51 were found almost an hour later, triggering a huge wave of speculation over the mystery object that had sent the airman plunging out of the sky to his death.

THE NARROW MARGIN

During my time with the Automobile Association, I had dealt with a considerable number of strange calls for assistance, but none more so than the one I took from a very frightened lady who was about to present the Association with a 'first' in motoring mishaps.

"Hello. A.A.? Can you help me? I've just had an accident."

As an opener, it guaranteed complete and immediate attention and I prepared to record the full details in anticipation of a relay recovery. Having established that nobody had been injured I asked for a rundown on the accident, to allow an assessment to be made for the type of recovery needed.

If the case itself was unique, the opening sentence certainly wasn't and could well have been coined with A.A. members in mind: "You aren't going to believe this, but..."

I listened carefully as the shaken driver sought to recall the moment of terror that led up to her accident.

"It was terrifying - I couldn't for the life of me make out what was happening. One minute I was driving happily down the Winchester by-pass, the next, a huge shadow fell across the car and this 'thing' came swooping out of the sky - right at me!"

As she paused for breath, I took the opportunity to attract a colleague's attention and indicated that he should start the ball rolling with regard to a patrol attendance as soon as possible. I then listened to the rest of the lady member's story.

"I've never seen anything like it in my life. It looked massive - I just knew it was going to crash into me I swerved to avoid a collision, but there was a tremendous bang and I felt the car swerve horribly. The next thing I remember is being helped out of my car by someone who'd seen me go off the road."

To find the connection between these two cases, it's necessary to look back at Captain Mantell's fatal encounter in 1948.

It was not until almost three years later that details of a secret experimental weather balloon, nicknamed 'Skyhook' became known to investigators. This massive balloon, capable of soaring high into the atmosphere, fitted the description of the Mantell UFO almost exactly and the mystery was finally laid to rest.

The cause of the crash was put down to the pilot blacking out through lack of oxygen whilst attempting to reach the balloon's staggering ceiling height.

The Winchester by-pass UFO, likewise, was a falling weather balloon, albeit not as large as a 'Skyhook model.

Accidents involving weather balloons are very rare and, although they are released into the atmosphere at regular intervals, it is generally acknowledged that they do not present a serious threat to life and limb. The two cases quoted are, unfortunately for the victims, the exceptions that prove the rule.

The weather will never cease to dominate our lives and seems intent on mocking all our attempts to forecast its intentions. It can produce breathtaking scenes of unparalleled beauty on the one hand, and cause devastating destruction on the other, yet we are dependent on its many vagaries for our very survival. I believe there are probably many more types of unknown weather phenomena and feel that new chapters in the UFO story will be written as and when they are eventually discovered. Until such time as this happens, the weather, like the UFO phenomenon itself, will continue to display only one predictable feature - its unpredictability!

FILE 7
A PERSONAL EXPERIENCE

Of all the questions put to me during the course of my investigations into UFOs, the one that crops up most frequently is, 'Have you ever seen one yourself?'

The answer, sadly, has to be no, I haven't - but I know a man who has!

To date, this is the only sighting that I have had a personal involvement with, and still ranks as one of my greatest memories, even though I missed the actual event.

To set the scene it is necessary to go back to Sunday, 16th April 1978. The time stood at 2200 hours and, along with my shift supervisor, Ted Godwin and crew mate, Len Middlewick, I had just booked on for the night shift at the A.A.'s Southampton Headquarters in Middle Street.

Our routine never varied when on nights. Ted took the Supervisor's chair alongside Len, who manned the phones and dealt with the garage call-outs. Meanwhile, I took over the radio from the off-going operator, slipped the headset on and adjusted the volume to my requirements.

We usually anticipated a busy couple of hours on a Sunday, and this particular night was no exception. The weather was fine and clear, and quite a few motorists were returning home after a weekend on the coast.

By midnight, we had a clear operations board and the majority of our breakdown patrols had signed off for the night. Only two remained. Tango Nine, patrolman Gilbert Reynolds, and Tango One-Two, patrolman Cyril Gates. Both men had considerable experience, and regularly worked the late shift to act as 'sweepers' for the odd breakdown that occurred after midnight. Their tour of duty ended at 0100.

At 0045 my headphones crackled into life.

"Southampton - Tango Nine. If it's all clear, I'm closing for the night."

"Roger Tango Nine, closing. Good night to you," I replied. One more to go and I could relax, take the headset off, set the radio on loudspeaker and make a cup of tea - our first break of the night. The remaining patrol, Cyril Gates, lived in Outlands Lane, Curdridge on the isolated eastern outskirts of Southampton. In common with most mechanics, he has a practical mind with little time for unexplained phenomena. His extrovert personality and outgoing sense of humour never failed to ignite our annual Christmas dance at an early hour, yet he was teetotal - a virtue he was to mention more than once in the months following.

At 0050 hours on Sunday 16th April 1978, Cyril Gates raised his hand-microphone to his lips and made a transmission that was to draw both of us into one of the most remarkable UFO encounters ever recorded on the South Coast.

"Southampton, a message. Tango One-Two over." The familiar radio preface filled my headphones.

"Tango One-Two pass" (your message), I answered. A slight pause followed, the crackling of static telling me that Tango One-Two's handmike button was still pressed down. The message, when it came, was calm and unhurried - although slightly hesitant.

"Southampton. Tango One-Two. I've just seen what you would probably call a UFO!"

"You've seen what?" I blurted, all radio procedure forgotten.

"A UFO," came the reply.

"Roger Tango One-Two, what location are you?" I asked, barely keeping the excitement out of my voice.

"Home base. I was about to sign off when I spotted it," answered the patrolman.

"Tango One-Two, understand home base. Can I landline (telephone) you for the details?" I queried.

"Affirmative, Southampton. Give me another two minutes to lock up."

"Cyril's just seen a UFO," I announced enthusiastically to Ted and Len as I took off my headset. "I'm going to give him a bell for the full story."

Both men looked at me silently for a few moments before reacting in their separate ways.

"I'll put the kettle on then," said Len. Ted merely took off his glasses, gave a long sigh that spoke volumes, and went back to his paperwork. Less than a minute later, I was talking to Cyril on the phone. This is his story:

"I'd just pulled into my driveway and climbed out of the van to open the garage doors," he started. "Out of the corner of my eye, I caught a glimpse of a bright light off to my left, over towards Botley Railway Station.

At that early hour, Outlands Lane and the surrounding countryside lay blanketed in darkness, a fact that served only to enhance the unusual aspect of the light source.

"I jumped up on to the bonnet of my van for a better view," continued the patrolman. "From there, I could see right over the railway station. The light seemed to be coming from behind a clump of trees."

He paused at my request, whilst I hurriedly scribbled down the details. A first-hand account of a UFO sighting within minutes of the actual event was not an everyday occurrence and I intended that the report should be as accurate as possible.

"Even as I looked," he continued, "This brilliantly lit, tadpole-shaped object rose slowly above the trees and hovered at around the same height as one of the electricity pylons nearby. It looked a sort of silvery-white colour and had a bulbous nose that tapered off into a tail." I interrupted once again and asked about the size of the object. As in many such cases, the witness used a familiar object to make his comparison.

"It was about the same size as one of our Relay transporters," he estimated. "It hovered over the railway station for a while and then started to move in my direction."

It was at this point that a sudden and startling move by the UFO lent a frightening edge to Cyril's sighting. "It just took-off," he recalled incredulously. "I've never seen anything like it in my life

before. It seemed to turn deliberately towards the east, and then just accelerated at a hell of a speed. It went past me at no more than 500 yards distance, climbing all the time. Orangey coloured sparks were flying from both sides of this thing as it shot by."

I ventured to suggest that it may have been a meteorite, but there was no doubt in the patrolman's mind. "I'd hardly think so," he replied, "Unless they're given to rising upwards from the ground and hovering before shooting off into the sky!"

He watched as the UFO disappeared over the skyline towards Portsmouth. What had been his feelings at the time?

"A little bit scared to tell the truth. I"d never believed this sort of thing before, but I'm convinced it was under some form of control, and if it was, it wasn't human control!"

I wanted to release the story to the press and asked Cyril if he minded. He had no objection, but expressed a fervent hope that he was not the only witness. He need not have worried. Unknown to either of us, other witnesses were indeed encountering the same UFO - even as we spoke!

Mrs. Josie Symonds, with husband Eric and two friends, had just arrived home after an evening out, and were just about to enter their

A.A. Patrolman Cyril Gates. His nocturnal duties gave him a close-up view of an extremely large, bright tadpole-shaped UFO that has never been explained.

home in Farlington, Portsmouth for a late cup of coffee. Eric was the first to spot the hurtling UFO coming in from the west, and pointed it out to the others. Josie recalled the eerie feeling that came over her as she watched the object's flight:

"I never thought in my life that I would see anything like that. It was a very bright light with what seemed like vapour forming a tail, making it tadpole-shaped. It didn't make a sound, yet it flew across Portsdown Hill at a fantastic speed. It really gave me the creeps and I shot indoors afterwards."

Ken Pratt, also of Farlington, was another witness who followed the path of the UFO as it blazed across the night sky.

"I was absolutely thunderstruck," he said, "It seemed like a dream and I just couldn't seem to move."

The mystery sphere then curved out over the water towards the Isle of Wight, where it was seen again before disappearing at an astonishing rate into the upper reaches of the night sky. The whole, amazing episode had lasted no longer than twelve minutes from original sightings to final departure.

Several local papers ran the story during the following week, and I submitted an article to our own A.A. newspaper, *Fanum News*. Cyril Gates achieved celebrity status among his colleagues and bore with stoicism a fair amount of good natured leg-pulling.

Only one incident really annoyed him, and this came from an unusual source. He told me about it shortly afterwards...

"I was enjoying my 'rest day' at home - doing a bit of gardening - when the phone rang," he said, "It was some professor from Bourne-mouth. Wanted to know all about my UFO."

This was an interesting development, and I waited with interest for the rest of the details. My involvement with UFO investigations was in its infancy at the time and I saw this as an exciting opportunity to establish contact with a far more experienced investigator.

"I told him exactly what I'd seen," continued Cyril, "He seemed really excited. He kept asking me if I"d seen anybody inside the UFO. In fact, he kept on about it so much I got the impression he was trying to make me believe I had seen figures. I got a bit annoyed over that, and told him I wasn't going to fabricate a story about spacemen for him or anybody else."

I groaned inwardly at this, as I could well imagine the outcome of such an interchange. Hoping against hope that some form of identification or address had been proffered at the outset, I asked the patrolman if he got the professor's phone number. "No I haven't," came the expected reply, "In fact, I can't even remember his name."

The conversation, it seemed, had ended rather abruptly. One snippet of information had emerged from the conversation though; in answer to a question about his own belief in UFOs, the well spoken professor had replied:

"It's not a question of 'belief'. UFOs do exist. It's as simple as that. Are they extra-terrestrial? Yes - there's no doubt about it!"

I went out to the sighting location the following week, to see if I could pick up any visual clues as to the object's size. Standing in Outlands Lane, I stared at the skies over Botley Railway Station - straight at a familiar landmark - electricity pylons - a whole row of them - stretching from the station towards Curdridge and beyond.

Could there be a connection? If St Elmo's Fire could fly off a ship's mast, could a ball of electricity do the same off a pylon? And if it could, would it then hover silently before accelerating away into space? Or could it have been a ball of discharged electricity from the power lines themselves travelling the entire length of the column of pylons? In the darkness this would certainly have given the impression that the 'UFO' was flying. I put these questions to the Central Electricity Generating Board, with a view to clarifying the situation:

"Very unlikely," replied a spokesman. "The pylons you mention, the smaller variety, carry 132,000 volts of electricity. Even if one of the top conductors received a direct lightning strike, the only effect it would have would be to bring in an automatic power cut-off. It certainly wouldn't produce a ball of electricity capable of flying upwards and detaching itself from the top of the pylon."

Discharged electricity, likewise, has never been known to travel - en-masse - along power lines, ruling out my second theory.

"There's only one type of unusual phenomenon associated with electricity pylons that we're aware of," I was informed. "A luminous white glow can sometimes be seen surrounding the pylon insulators. We call it 'corona discharge' - small light particles that are generated by a combination of static, humidity and dust."

Perhaps there's a possibility that 'corona discharge' may have been responsible for some of Hampshire's UFO sightings, but certainly not this one. The glow from the discharge remains stationary for the duration of its existence, and in size it's only slightly larger than the insulator itself. It bears no similarity at all to the massive sphere of moving light seen by the A.A. man.

The experts could offer no other explanation for the light source. Any lingering doubts they may have had, with regard to an unknown electrical phenomenon making its dazzling debut, were quickly dispelled when I mentioned the object's size.

"It would be quite impossible," I was told, "for a ball of electricity of that magnitude to form on one of our pylons, let alone fly off it and shoot away into space!" There

seemed no logical explanation for the sighting and, to this day, no satisfactory conclusion has ever been reached. If, as the patrolman stated, the object appeared to be under control, who do we look to as the controllers? He could see no sign of life or even anything that resembled a cockpit, so do we look at the possibility of remote control? If this seems a feasible alternative, then the likelihood that the object was returning from whence it came cannot be overlooked. As the UFO was last seen streaking into space, is it really so absurd to suggest that the controlling intelligence behind it could also have been from beyond earth?

During a quiet moment with the patrolman a few days after the sighting, I asked him if he thought the UFO was extraterrestrial.

Something in his reply has stuck in my mind ever since:

"I don't know. I can't accept that they wouldn't make contact with us if they've come all this way, but then again, there's a passage in the Bible that I believe refers to other planets and civilisations."

Intrigued, I asked for the quotation. The answer was short, only four words, yet they held the promise of life elsewhere.

"Many worlds have I."

FILE 8
THE PORTSMOUTH EPISODE

The vast majority of UFO sightings in Hampshire are concentrated around its coastal towns and cities - a fact that may have a direct bearing on their close proximity to the sea (several ufologists support the theory that UFOs are capable of extensive underwater activity).

One such city is Portsmouth...

Steeped in naval history, this legendary seaport seems an unlikely location for UFO visitations, yet the facts speak for themselves.

In 1978, for instance, whilst driving down a lonely road on the top of Portsdown Hill, a Porchester family met with a huge, flying object that brought terror in its passing.

The time stood at 1900 hours on the 7th November as Kevin Malling drove carefully down Nelson Lane, his car headlights piercing the gloom of a chill water's night. In the car with him, his wife, Lynn, daughter, Karen (6) and son, Kevin (5), were looking forward to a warm fire and a hot drink in the comfort of their own home.

"As I drove down Nelson Lane, I spotted a bright light hovering over a ploughed field ahead of us," said Kevin, "As I drew closer I could make out this huge, mushroom shaped object. It had a brilliant white light on top - as powerful as a searchlight."

By now the whole family were staring in amazement at the unidentified aero-form as it hung silently over the cultivated field.

"We could see two banks of lights at the bottom of the object - red on top, green below," recalled Kevin. "I just watched in utter disbelief. We were all stunned and shocked - the kids were really frightened."

They were drawing level with the field when the UFO began to move slowly across and in front of them, very low down.

"I was still moving forward," recalled Kevin, "When this thing suddenly moved right over us!"

Fully aware that they were directly beneath the unknown object and unsure of its intentions, the frightened family could only watch and wait.

"It was absolutely petrifying," revealed Kevin, "The eerie thing about it was the total lack of noise. For something that big to be so silent was beyond belief."

As they strove frantically to keep sight of the UFO it re-appeared, accelerating rapidly towards Fareham.

"It just shot across the sky in seconds," said Kevin, "I've never seen anything so big move as fast as that thing!"

Badly shaken by their ordeal, the family continued with their journey and arrived, with a feeling of great relief, back home in Porchester.

Accepting that details of their experience would meet with a great deal of scepticism, Kevin and Lynn Malling nevertheless reported their sighting. Kevin summed up the episode with a statement that, with variations, crops up time and again during the course of UFO investigations.

" I know the story sounds far-fetched. I'd think so too if it were told to me, but that's exactly what we saw."

It was suggested that a hot-air balloon may have been responsible for the Malling's incredible encounter and, at first glance, this seemed a possible solution. In size, at least, there was a definite similarity between the two. Attention was also drawn to the absence of noise during the object's flight - another indication, surely, of its true identity - but was it?

The roar of a hot-air burner as it blast out waves of heat can be clearly heard above most ground noises, so it's hard to believe that the Malling's would have failed to hear anything, even over the noise made by their car's engine.

The flare from the burner would have also been very noticeable in the darkness, a beacon of recognisable normality, but no flames were seen.

Then there was the object's speed. Even the most fervent enthusiast would find difficulty in explaining why a wind-propelled hot-air balloon could suddenly find the power to "shoot across the sky in seconds."

It is also possible that the UFO was an unknown experimental device. Portsmouth is bristling with military establishments and the sighting took place very near the Admiralty Research Establishment on Portsdown Hill. Unsurprisingly, they denied any knowledge of the object. It certainly was not the first time this secret installation had been drawn into the controversy and, on one memorable occasion, it was the focal point of an incident that sparked a major alert! (see File 9).

The Malling's extraordinary encounter took place at a time when UFO activity appeared to be peaking out on top of the '70s 'wave'. No credible solution has been put forward. The sighting has yet to be satisfactorily explained.

Four years later, Portsdown Hill provided the setting for another, equally baffling, sighting.

Principle witness, Paul Edwards of Waterlooville, described the object he saw on the night of 13th December 1982.

"It was a perfect circle of bright light, moving very fast. I'd say it was about 1,000ft up," he estimated.

"There was a peculiar humming sound coming from it and, at first, I thought it could have been a satellite breaking up."

However, he quickly dismissed this explanation as he followed the object's trajectory. "It had no tail at all behind it, and looked to be something far more than just a piece of burnt out satellite."

Fifteen-year-old Colin New, of Bedhampton, also witnessed the object's flight and confirmed Paul's description.

"I was half way through my paper round when a bright light over Portsdown Hill caught my eye," he remembered. "I looked up and saw this fantastic flying circle shooting past."

THE ASTRONOMER'S SIGHTING

Astronomers are usually a mine of information when it comes to explaining mysterious aerial lights, and many high-altitude sightings have been solved by a quick phone call to one of these 'celestial' experts.

Sometimes, however, even the best of them are faced with the unexplainable...

On the night of July 3rd 1984, Portsmouth astronomers rushed to focus their telescopes on a bright star, high in the night sky. They had been alerted by fellow observer, Graham Boots of Worthing, who had noted an irregularity in the star's setting.

"I thought, at first, that it was a nova (super-bright star) but soon realised it couldn't have been," he told reporters from the 'Portsmouth News'.

"I worked out its height at around 25 miles and, for the life of me, I couldn't identify it." The object remained in view for almost twenty minutes before departing in spectacular fashion...

"It suddenly split in two and vanished from sight," said an astonished Graham. Astronomers all along the south coast, who had witnessed the startling event, admitted to being baffled - even the Royal Greenwich Observatory was at a loss to offer an explanation.

Artificial satellites? Meteors? Aircraft? All were ruled out by the knowledgeable stargazers. In desperation, they turned to famous astronomer, Patrick Moore, a local man from nearby Selsey. If anyone could solve this unusual mystery, surely he could.

Well-known for his scepticism on the subject of UFOs, the 'Sky at Night' man nonetheless admitted to being stumped for an answer on this occasion.

"In the ordinary way, I'm extremely sceptical about reports of UFOs" he stated, "but this light was seen by people who are good amateur astronomers and who know what they are doing."

Astronomers are not usually at a loss to explain away the irregular antics of high-altitude lightforms, which makes this sighting exceptional. It is also one of the very few LITS observations that has rated an 'Origin Unknown' label.

Over the last twenty years or so, Portsmouth has produced a rich crop of UFO encounters, many of them truly baffling. The incredible 'bands of light' incident in September 1981 for instance...

The first sighting took place on a deserted back-road near the village of Westbourne, a quiet country retreat that lies midway between Chichester and Portsmouth. The time was 9.30pm.

Two local men, Oliver Mann and Anthony Stewart were the first to spot the object as it hurtled low across Westbourne Common.

Startled by its sudden appearance, both men stopped to watch as it drew nearer, expecting to see a low-flying jet. Instead, they witnessed a brilliant circular device, the like of which they had never seen before.

"It looked just like two bands of lights, very wide, one on top of the other," said Oliver. "I couldn't say exactly how fast it was going, but it was certainly shifting.

"The light bands looked as though they may have been part of a single object, the middle section unlit. We finally lost sight of it as it disappeared towards Portsmouth.

At the same time as the two Westbourne men were following the object's departure, Mrs Ruth Smith and two friends were driving along Southwick Road in Portsmouth's Denmead area.

"We were on our way to Water-looville," explained Ruth. "It was pitch black on that stretch of road, so we weren't going very fast at the time."

Two pinpoints of light suddenly appeared in the rear view mirror, rapidly growing larger.

"I pointed them out to my friends," said Ruth, "They were very bright, like two circles, one on top of the other. They came streaking up behind us, very low down, and overtook us on the right hand side. I'd say they were about a field's distance away."

Instead of flying straight on, the lights suddenly changed direction. "They banked right over and flew across the road in front of us - it was amazing," recalled Ruth. "We watched until it vanished in the distance."

Both parties were able to compare notes a few days later, and it quickly became obvious that the two sightings had been of the same object. All later attempts at identification (and there were many), failed!

"Why, if so many UFOs have been seen over Hampshire, are there so few, decent photographs available. Surely at least one of the witnesses had a camera handy?"

This question, a perfectly reasonable one, came from a colleague of mine who happens to be a very gifted photographer, who would not dream of going anywhere without his camera primed and ready for that unexpected scoop.

The answer, of course, is that we are not all ace photographers. Very few people keep a camera permanently to hand and even those who do are not necessarily experts.

On more than one occasion, witnesses have told me that they did have a camera available, but, for one reason or another, failed to use it.

"It was all over in a matter of seconds," said one, "I never had the chance to even think about taking a photograph."

"It wouldn't have mattered if I'd had a loaded camera in my hand," said another, "I was so bloody scared that I'd have probably dropped it anyway."

"It was at night and I wasn't sure if my camera could take photos in the dark," said a third.

Sometimes, however, there will be a photographer in the right place, at the right time. On the 3rd April 1978, Havant engineer, Richard Burkatt, found himself in just the right place - H.M.S. *Vernon*, Portsmouth. The time stood at 9.00pm exactly.

"I'd been taking some evening view of Portsmouth, and had decided to finish off the session by loosing off a few shots of Vernon," he remembered. "Everything went quite well and I was looking forward to developing the film the next day."

Engrossed in his work, Richard noticed nothing unusual at the time he was taking the photographs. The mystery was not to present

An amazing photograph of a strange looking craft. Attempts to prove the photograph a fake have so far failed (photo Southampton Evening Echo).

itself until the following day... "I'd just finished developing the film, when I noticed something strange on one of the Vernon prints," recalled Richard. "A three-cornered flying object appeared to be hovering over the base, though how on earth I failed to see it at the time, I'll never know."

A thorough check of the negatives showed no obvious defects and none of the other prints were affected.

Puzzled by the clearly defined object, he decided to contact the *Portsmouth News*. If they would include the photograph in one of their editions, surely someone would spot it and come up with an explanation.

It was at this stage that the final, dramatic twist came. A few hours before Richard Birkatt rang them, the *News* had received a call from a Portsmouth couple who, from their 12th floor flat, had seen a "three-cornered UFO" descend swiftly out of the sky and pass directly over H.M.S. *Vernon*. The sighting had taken place the previous night, the same night that Richard had been taking his photographs. The time? 9.00pm!

Portsdown Hill has featured prominently in several quite extraordinary UFO encounters in

Portsmouth, and it seems only fitting to return, once again, to its mysterious heights to record the final sighting in this chapter - a sighting that saw yet another inexplicable object overflying the city's most prominent landmark.

DECEMBER 9TH 1980. 8.30pm

The object first appeared as a point of red light, low in the night sky, approaching from the Petersfield direction. For Chris Harrison, a Portsmouth man, it appeared, at first, to be one of the multitude of stars and planets that were visible in the cloudless winter sky.

"I soon realised it was no star," recalled Chris, "It was growing bigger by the second as it drew closer and I could see a bright red glow coming from inside the object."

Round in shape, and very large, the UFO passed silently over Chris's vantage point, revealing another startling feature as it did so.

"There were bright green flashes shooting out of the back end, just like miniature forks of lightning. It was unbelievable." said Chris. "Suddenly, the red glow seemed to intensify and the object began to pick up speed rapidly. I last saw it shooting off towards Portsdown Hill."

Portsmouth will forever be associated with the sea and ships; with historic voyages of discovery and famous naval heroes. Throughout its long history, thousands of sailors of all nationalities have brought ashore spellbinding tales of great sea mysteries. Can we now expect the City of Portsmouth, will its recent history of UFO visitations, aerial apparitions and shimmering spheroids, to take its place amongst the best of them?

FILE 9
VEIL OF SECRECY

Clearly outlined against the sky on top of Portsdown Hill, the Admiralty Research Establishment looks oddly out of place alongside the crumbling ruins of nearby Fort Southwick - its modern radar scanner providing a marked contrast to the fort's ancient cannon.

Harbouring a vast labyrinth of underground laboratories and workshops, its scientists and technicians are constantly engaged on top-secret projects in the field of underwater weapons research, and electronic warfare. At the time of this dramatic and chilling incident in March 1960, it was known as A.S.W.E. (Admiralty Surface Weapons Establishment).

Walking over the bridge linking Stoke Road to Forton Road in Gosport, Ernie Sears sought to avoid the worse of a strong gale by turning slightly sideways to lessen the effect of the headwind. As he turned, a bright shard of light in the early morning sky over Portsdown Hill, caught his eye. Pausing to take a closer look, he saw a stationary object, very bright, hovering over the A.S.W.E.

Puzzled by the cigar-shaped aero-form, but thinking it was probably a slow moving aeroplane battling against the strong winds, he turned to carry on across the bridge. From the other end, in an obvious hurry, a young man was approaching him.

"I stopped him as he drew level," Ernie told me. "I pointed out the object and asked him if he thought it was an aeroplane. He glanced quickly towards it, said 'Yes' and dashed off.

In no less of a hurry himself, Ernie settled for this explanation, and carried on about his business.

Approximately twenty to thirty minutes later, in another part of Gosport, he heard the fast approaching roar of low flying jet aircraft.

"The noise was deafening," he recalled, "I knew they must have been very low."

Dashing into the street, he was just in time to see two Meteor jet fighters sweep past - climbing rapidly towards Portsdown Hill!

"I looked beyond the two jets and saw the same object I'd seen earlier, still hovering over the A.S.W.E. I knew then, that it was no ordinary aircraft that I'd seen," he stated.

The two fighters, at maximum

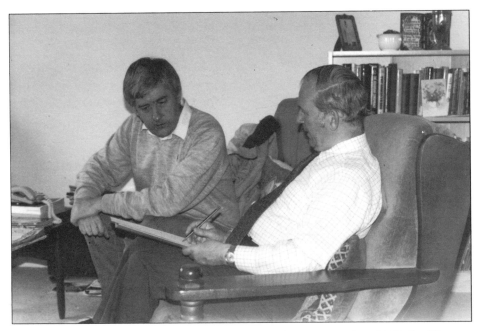

Ernest Sears describing his UFO sighting over the ARE facility at Portsdown Hill to author, Bob Price. Mr Sears witnessed the interception of the UFO by two RAF jets, an incident later denied by the Air Force.

thrust, were closing in on the mystery craft with lightning speed. Ernie, enthralled could only stand and watch as the dramatic events unfolded above him.

Suddenly, as though detecting the fighter's presence, the object turned on end - and vanished!

"It was unbelievable," said Ernie. "It just disappeared, like a light bulb going out. One second it was there, turning slowly on end in a smooth controlled manner, the next, it was gone!"

The fighters circled above the Establishment for several minutes before finally breaking off and heading back in the direction of RAF Thorney Island.

Running to the nearest telephone box, Ernie quickly found the air base's telephone number and rang in, asking to speak to the control tower duty officer.

"I knew. from my own service experience, that military aircraft were never 'scrambled' over built-up areas unless there was an emergency," he said, "so it was obvious that something serious had sparked a major alert."

After a lengthy wait, he was eventually put through, and spoke to the duty officer.

"I asked if he could identify the object I'd seen over Portsdown Hill, and if he could explain why the two Meteor jets were chasing it," said Ernie. "I'll never forget his answer as long as I live. He said, quite coldly, 'You didn't see any object and you didn't see any Meteor jets either!' I began to protest, but he just repeated what he'd said and ended the conversation."

Mystified and alarmed though he was, by this sinister turn of events, he realised there was little he could do about it. Any further attempts to glean information from the military would, inevitably, be met with a flat denial. To report the incident to the newspapers would, he felt, serve no useful purpose. Resigned to the fact that he would probably never know the origin of the Portsdown UFO, Ernie Sears was not to know that the following day would reveal one more tantalising piece of unusable evidence to support his claim that something strange and frightening had indeed happened over the A.S.W.E.

"My brother-in-law, an electrical draughtsman working at the Establishment at the time, had just popped in for a cup of tea and a chat," said Ernie, recalling the events of the following day. "As he came through the door, I quite casually said, 'You had a bit of excitement at your place yesterday, didn't you?' He stopped in mid-stride, and the colour just drained out of his face - he went absolutely white. It was obvious I"d touched a very raw nerve, and I immediately dropped the subject, but it was all I needed to convince me that a major 'scare' had occurred the previous day," Ernie concluded.

If we are to accept that 'genuine' UFOs exist, (and by 'genuine' I mean controlled craft) as a great deal of the evidence suggests, then we must also accept that they are technically far superior to any man-made flying machine in existence today.

As such it is hardly surprising that attempts at interception by fighter aircraft usually fail. This frustrating fact, despite vigorous Government denials, has not stopped them trying!

In the early 1950s, the pilot of a Canberra aircraft, flying high over the Hampshire/Wiltshire border, detected a blip on his radar screen, indicating that a 'target' was tailing him at a range of approximately five miles. Retired Wing Commander, Cyril Townsend-Withers, whose sighting was investigated by the Manchester UFO Research Association, takes up the story...

"I was the passenger on this occasion," he explained. "When the blip came up on the screen, I went up into the viewing turret and saw this brightly lit object coming up behind us. We tried to shake it

Two remarkable UFO photographs from a series taken in 1989 show a spheroid object over Southampton.

off, without success, so my pilot swung us round to face it."

As they approached head-on, he could see that the object was about the size of a small fighter, with, what appeared to be small stabilising fins at the rear.

"All of a sudden, this object just rocketed away in a vertical climb," claimed the Wing Commander. "It must have reached 70,000ft in seconds."

Again, during the 1970s 'wave', a Winchester schoolboy, Tim Robinson, witnessed yet another desperate attempt by fighters to close with a UFO.

"I heard the jet first and looked up to see what sort they were," he said. "The looked like Lightnings - two of them - going at a fantastic speed. They were chasing a funny, 'mushroom' shaped object."

Tim concentrated on the UFO as it streaked across the sky.

"I couldn't see any lights or exhaust or anything like that," he said, "but it was going much faster than the two Lightnings and when it finally shot up into the clouds, it seemed to be pulling right away from them."

One question hangs over these earnest pursuits, widely believed to be carried out by fully-armed fighter aircraft.

What action, if any, would the pilots take if they ever caught-up with one of these UFOs? We'll never know the answer, of course, until it happens in front of witnesses. If the RAF has an action plan for UFO intercepts, it's certainly not going to make it public. As far as I am aware, nobody here has yet accused the RAF of undue aggression against unidentified flying objects - unlike the citizens of other countries, most notably America.

Major Donald Keyhoe, for instance, in his book *Aliens from Space*, not only accused the Aerospace Defence Command of instructing fighter pilots to shoot down UFOs, but also quoted a case where shots were actually fired...

An F80 fighter, at top speed, had managed to close to within five hundred yards of a saucer-shaped metallic UFO. As it started to accelerate away from him, the F80 pilot armed his guns and fired a long, but ineffectual, burst at the departing UFO.

If it seems unthinkable that any Government could give standing orders that would allow the shooting down of a possibly friendly craft on a peaceful mission, then consider these facts.

The long-running arms race between the super powers is showing no signs of slowing down despite the recent thaw in East/

West relations. Genuine, but relatively small, cut-backs by Soviet and American governments do nothing to disguise the fact that both are still striving desperately to hold the 'better' hand. The United States refuse point-blank to abandon their 'Star-Wars' project, despite strong Russian protests, because they know it will give them a massive lead on their rivals.

Supposing, in the midst of this battle for supremacy, an opportunity arose to shoot down and study a flying machine of such an advanced design that it could easily render obsolete, every aircraft and weapon so far devised by man.

Remote though such a possibility may seem, it certainly cannot be ruled out altogether. As such, it is not unreasonable to assume that defence chiefs have already considered the implications and laid down certain guidelines for use in the event of a close (aerial) encounter.

If any country could lay its hands on the secrets of a genuine UFO propulsion unit, the advantages it could gain in the arms race would be immeasurable.

Sadly, it may be a temptation they could not resist!

What of the British Government's attitude towards UFOs? A great deal of criticism has been levelled at the Ministry of Defence for their alleged 'cover-up' policy, but is it justified? Are they withholding vital information concerning the reality of UFOs or are they genuinely innocent of the charges brought against them by frustrated investigators? A look at the evidence will allow you to form your own opinion...

On the 18th January 1979, the Earl of Clancarty (Brinsley LePoer Trench) rose to open a debate in the House of Lords. The session, about UFOs, lasted almost four hours. In his opening speech, he called on Lord Strabogli, who was to speak on behalf of the Government, to contact the Secretary of State for Defence with a view to appearing on television to reveal the known facts about UFO encounters in Great Britain.

The Earl pointed out the example set by French Defence Minister, Robert Galley who, in a nationwide radio broadcast in 1974, had publicly acknowledged the reality of UFOs and confirmed the existence of a special unit responsible solely for the collation of UFO sighting reports.

In a twenty-five minute reply, Lord Strabogli sought to systematically explain away the many quoted sightings as natural phenomena or mis-identifications. He also assured the House that there was no Government 'cover-up' and, as such, felt that little would be achieved by the appearance on television, of the Secretary of State for Defence. Needless to say, no such appearance ever took place.

It should be pointed out that more was undoubtedly read into the French Minister's radio broadcast than was originally intended. Lord Strabogli had taken the precaution of reading the transcript of Minister Galley's broadcast, and found that he had conceded only the reality of the UFO 'phenomena' - not, as many ufologists were happy to believe, the existence of UFOs as extraterrestrial spaceships.

If Lord Strabogli's interpretation of the speech is correct, then the British Government has no case to answer. They have never denied the existence of the 'phenomena', and make no secret of the fact that thousands of sighting reports are received by them every year. What then, is the MoD's official stance on UFOs?

On the 23rd May 1989, I received the following letter from Whitehall, in answer to this question....

Dear Sir,

I have been asked to reply to your recent letter in which you asked a number of questions about the Ministry of Defence's attitude to UFOs. The answers are as follows:

1. The sole concern of the Ministry of Defence is to ensure that the reports we receive do not present a threat to the security and defence of the United Kingdom. The Ministry does not attempt to investigate reported sightings unless a threat is identified. NO such cases have ever been identified.

2. The Ministry has no department which is appointed solely for the purpose of studying UFO reports. Reports are referred to MoD Air Defence staffs, who examine them as part of their normal duties. Because of our limited involvement with this particular subject, we do not, nor do we have any need to, interview individuals who might have witnessed an unusual incident. Indeed, unless we judge that a sighting poses a threat, and this has not been the case so far, the MoD does not attempt to investigate or identify whatever might have been seen.

3. The MoD maintains a policy of keeping all sighting reports received. Regrettably, because of lack of resources, we are unable to initiate general surveys or searches through our files. You may be aware that all MoD files are subject to the Public Records Act, which means that after closure they remained closed from public viewing for 30 years. However, we are able to answer any specific queries you may have about particular incidents which may have occurred recently and can let you know whether we have a report on the incident and, if so, what it contained.

In conclusion, I can say that the very vast majority of sightings have a terrestrial explanation (including the UFO Kite flying club). The MoD does not possess any positive evidence that 'alien spacecraft' have landed on this planet.

Yours etc....

This letter leaves little room for doubt concerning the MoD's 'official' attitude to the UFO phenomena, yet several question marks hang over some of the issues raised.

In paragraph 2, emphasis is placed on the fact that no department is appointed solely with the task of studying UFO reports, yet in October 1988, an incident occurred that cast a great deal of doubt on this statement.

Investigators contacting the MoD with UFO reports are usually put through to the RAF's Air Staff 2 department, who are often able to compare sightings with aircraft movement in the area concerned.

Michael Hanson, southern area representative for the Yorkshire UFO Society, had made many such calls and, on the day in question, had just finished speaking to the department with regard to a sighting report he'd received earlier in the day.

"They weren't able to help on this particular occasion," he recalled, "but for some reason, they told me to hang on while they put me through to DI55 (Defence Intelligence 55).

The initial transfer call was answered and the department was definitely identified.

"Unfortunately, I identified myself straight away," said Michael. "There was a long pause, then I suddenly found myself back with the switchboard operator, who told me that no one was available."

In an effort to solve the mystery, he rang back later in the day and asked to be put through to DI55. "The operator told me there was no such department," said Michael. "When I mentioned that I'd been speaking to them earlier, I was told, in no uncertain terms, that I shouldn't have been put through!"

Several prominent ufologists are convinced that this secret department exists. Timothy Good, author of *Above Top Secret*, is one of them. He claims to have documented evidence that top-level investigations into UFO incidents have been taking place since the 1950s.

Paragraph 2 of the Ministry's letter also states, '...we do not, nor do we have any need to, interview individuals who might have witnessed an unusual incident.'

This statement may come as a surprise to Police Constable Len Haffenden, (see File 2) who spent almost three-quarters of an hour on the telephone being closely questioned by a senior RAF intelligence officer who displayed more than a passing interest in his experience. Telephone interviews, it seems, do not count.

The letter ends in a somewhat caustic tone by insisting that the MoD is not in possession of any positive evidence that 'alien spacecraft' have landed on Earth - but has it already hidden away the greatest find in the history of Ufology? Have we already seen the arrival on our planet of an extra-terrestrial space probe, small and unmanned though it may have been? One man who had the answer was Lord Dowding, Commander-in-Chief of Fighter Command during the Battle of Britain.

During a visit to Hampshire in May 1959, he told fellow Rotarians that he had actually held a small, saucer-shaped object that had crashed to earth on the Yorkshire Moors.

Describing the object, he said it was approximately four feet in diameter and appeared to be made of an extremely tough, copper-like metal. Consisting of two separate halves, it defied all attempts to prise it open. Finally oxyacetylene cutters were employed and, with great difficulty, the object was eventually opened. To the great excitement of everyone at the scene, a book, bound in the same metallic material was found inside. The book was packed with strange hieroglyphics, unlike any language found on Earth!

If this amazing claim is true, and judging by the undoubted integrity of the source, there is no reason to suppose that it is not, then where is this book today? Has it been made a subject of the Public Records Act and filed away for thirty years? If this is the case, can we now expect it to be released for public scrutiny in the near future?

The thought of a 'flying saucer' travelling millions of miles through space on a mission designed to impart knowledge to other planets may seem preposterous. It is also asking a great deal to expect to find a planet as small as ours and then avoid crashing into the vast expanse of sea that covers most of its surface. But what if it was not the only one?

Thee was nothing particularly elaborate about the object or its contents - two sections of metal housing a book - so is it possible that thousands, or even millions may have been launched in a random attempt to contact any inhabited planet? I am happy to acknowledge that even a million of these tiny probes could travel forever in the vastness of space without finding a home, but I am also a great believer in remarkable coincidences...

Several years ago, scientists discovered that a dog killed by a chunk of space debris had been hit by a piece of the planet Mars! The odds on a piece of rock flying off the planet and hitting Earth in the first place, are staggering. For it to strike such a small and seemingly innocent object as the unfortunate dog is beyond belief - yet it happened.

Remember also, that our own Voyager 2 spacecraft is now flying into deep space after a five billion mile journey that has now taken it beyond the edge of our own solar system. Packed with information about our planet's location, its inhabitants and cultures, Voyager is Earth's pathfinder to the stars. Is it, as the Government would have us believe, all one-way traffic? I think not!

In August 1988, reports of a UFO sighting by two Chandlers Ford women appeared in local Southampton newspapers. The sighting itself, of a brightly lit aeroform was not particularly noteworthy, but the events that followed were to prove both intriguing and alarming.

Mrs Margaret Harris and Mrs Margaret Wilson had spotted the UFO whilst driving from Christchurch to Chandlers Ford.

"It was like a bright, white and yellow light hovering over the car," recalled Mrs Harris, "it was something very strange that I couldn't explain - it had no real shape that I could describe."

Mrs Wilson, who was in the passenger seat, managed to take several photographs of the object and, on reaching home, immediately 'phoned the police to report the incident.

Aware that the press would be informed, Mrs Wilson was not unduly alarmed when a man claiming to be a 'reporter' called at her house and asked if he could take the film away to be developed.

She handed the film over, on the understanding that the prints would be returned to her as soon as possible, and she was satisfied at the time, that she could easily get in touch with the man or his newspaper.

"That's the last I ever saw of him or the film," said Mrs Wilson ruefully.

Acting on her behalf, a solicitor sought to track down the 'reporter'. His findings? "I believe he is either an unscrupulous ufologist prepared to poach anything, or a member of some secret organisation, possibly with Government connections," he told real reporters.

Neither the man, nor the film has ever been found!

There has long been a suspicion amongst the various UFO organisations, that the Government has been responsible for the disappearance of the original UFO related photographs and documents submitted to them for analysis. Many claim that they do not always wait for the evidence to be submitted but, as in the case above, instigate an immediate enquiry.

The 'cover-up' conspiracy will continue to be a highly emotive subject amongst ufologists. The Government will be accused of withholding information, as it has been for decades; the MoD will continue to field the barrage of searching questions thrown at it concerning their involvement.

We must cling to the hope that somewhere and at sometime an encounter is waiting to happen that will forever break the veil of secrecy surrounding the greatest mystery of modern times.

FILE 10
THE CROPFIELD CIRCLES

Worldwide attention has recently been focused on the heart of the Hampshire Countryside, where a strange, and relatively new phenomenon has emerged to baffle scientists and laymen alike - the Crop Circles.

The circles, flattened swirls of matured cereal crops (wheat, barley, oil seed rape, etc.), first came to the notice of an astonished public in 1981, when a set of three were discovered in a field located within the 'Devil's Punchbowl' at Cheesefoot Head, near Winchester.

Consisting of a large centre circle flanked by two smaller 'satellite' rings, they appeared to be inch-perfect in their spacings, and perfectly round in shape.

The absence of any marks in the surrounding corn led to the inevitable conclusion that they could only have been formed by the downward pressure of something descending from above. Swiftly latching on to the fact that the 'something' must have been circular in shape, the media were quick to promote the theory that they were caused by UFOs - a theory strongly supported by the British UFO Society. They believed, and still do, that the circles were UFO 'nests', made by the materialisation of extraterrestrial vehicles. Others, (and there are many) disagree.

Many of the farmers put the blame for the damage, estimated to run into hundreds of pounds, on vandals.

"Wanton damage," claimed Lt. Commander Henry Bruce, owner of the affected field, "We must have lost a good acre of corn."

How the hoaxers managed to create the circles whilst leaving the rest of the corn untouched, however, remained a mystery. In later years, tractor wheel-marks were used to disguise the stealthy approach of various pranksters, but on this occasion, only a few, very faint, tracks were visible. They certainly weren't heavy enough to cover the approach of anyone on foot.

An equally mysterious discovery ruled out the hoax theory. All of the corn, flattened and swirled in a clockwise direction, was completely intact! There was no evidence to suggest that a human being had set foot inside the circles at any time! Other theories followed thick and fast.

"Mating hedgehogs or rutting deer," claimed some 'countrymen' experts, with witty tongues firmly in their cheeks."Druid ceremonies," suggested others.

Helicopters were suggested, and here, at last, seemed a reasonable explanation for the phenomenon. The swirling downwash of a helicopter's main rotor blades would surely account for the neat, circular pattern found in the cropfield. The tail rotor, it was felt, would create the smaller rings.

"Not so, " said an aviation expert after examining the evidence. "For a helicopter to cause that sort of damage, it would have to fly upside-down, and remain absolutely stationary." Moreover, experiments by the BBC have proved beyond all doubt that helicopters could not have created the desired effect.

The mystery deepened as, year after year, the circles defied all attempts at identification - mocking, it seemed, man's inability to reach into the unknown. Was there, after all, something to be said for the UFO theory...?

DATELINE: 6TH JULY 1985. TIME: 2300 HOURS

For Jack and Pat Collins, a Winchester couple, the drive home along the A272 from Stockbridge was just another routine, slightly boring journey - the price they were happy to pay for a pleasant evening out. There was very little traffic to impede their progress and, as they drew level with Stockbridge Down, Jack remarked that another half an hour should see them enjoying a bedtime drink in the safety of their own home.

A bright light, hovering low over the downs, drew Jack's attention.

"It was like a perfect circle and extremely bright," he told investigators. Pat, being in the passenger's seat was able to study the object a little closer.

"It looked just like a fairground wheel with lights around the rim, and spokes in the middle," she recalled.

Jack reported his sighting to the police, but nothing was found by the officers who attended the scene.

However, the following day, a 'crop circle' was found at Goodworth Clatford, just a few short miles of the spot where Jack and Pat Collins had seen the hovering, circular-shaped UFO!

Several investigations into the circles phenomenon were well underway at the time of this sighting, and a far wider picture was beginning to emerge. Reports had been compiled from as far afield as Australia, Russia, Brazil and the U.S.A - some with accompanying UFO sightings. Several of the British reports dated

The perfection of crop circles such as this one, discovered in a Hampshire wheatfield, is typical of this extraordinary phenomenon.

as far back as 1918, highlighting the fact that the circles certainly are not a product of the space-age or an early example of the 'greenhouse effect,'

Ranging from single to complex five-ring formations, the circles displayed some extraordinary features...

Some of the ringed circles, for instance, had counter-rotating swirls of corn, whilst one, rare, double-ringed set found at Cheesefoot Head provided an even bigger mystery. The centre circle swirled clockwise, in opposition to the first ring, which lay in an anti-clockwise spiral. The outer ring completed the bizarre pattern by reversing back to a clockwise swirl!

The case for the UFO theory strengthened in 1987, when a Winchester newspaper gave a detailed account of an incident that took place at Cheesefoot Head in the summer of 1980.

A local man, out walking his dog, had apparently heard a mysterious humming sound coming from the vicinity of a nearby cornfield. Deciding to investigate, he came across more than he bargained for...

"The noise was something like a combine harvester," he told

It is not only in standing crops that mysterious circles are found. In this aerial view of the Hampshire countryside a dark circular patch in the field below the carriageway may also suggest a UFO landing site.

reporters, "but the object I saw in that field was like nothing on Earth. It was a grey, spaceship-like object, floating slowly across the top of the corn.:"

He claimed that the UFO then settled gently on to the ground, and remained there for approximately five minutes. When it took off again, a perfect circle was left in its wake!

This belated report lost much of its initial impact when several contradictory statements were made by the witness during the course of two separate investi-gations. He may, of course, have simply been confused - the time lapse between the original sighting, and the eventual disclosure, was considerable. Whatever the truth behind this startling encounter, investigators felt that little was to be gained, at that late stage, from the pursuance of further enquiries into the Cheesefoot Head UFO and its possible link with the circles phenomenon.

What else then, could explain the strange and beautiful rings that were now appearing every year on the hills and downs of rural

Hampshire? Extensive and thorough research was the obvious requirement.

As previously mentioned, several investigations were already underway, but opinions were divided as to the possible cause of the mystery. The British UFO Society (BUFOS), convinced as to the extraterrestrial nature of the phenomenon, were quick to link three linear circles, discovered at Cheesefoot Head in 1981, with the ancient monuments at Stonehenge.

The monuments lay in a straight line between the three circles, and Westbury in Wiltshire, where several circles had also materialised. The size and dimensions of the monolithic

Stonehenge circles were found to be very similar to many of the cropfield variety. Coincidence - or a clue to the mystery?

A best-selling book, *Circular Evidence* came out of the vast dossier of information compiled by two Hampshire men, Pat Delgado and Colin Andrews - founders of the Circles Phenomenon Research Group. Their long search for a satisfactory explanation makes fascinating and for some, controversial reading.

Unlike the BUFOS approach to the problem however, they refuse to accept any one theory as the probable culprit, and seek to investigate the phenomenon in a fair and open-minded manner. On

This news photograph, taken at Cheesefoot Head near Winchester, clearly shows a pair of ring circles. Natural phenomena or signs of a UFO landing? (photo Southern Newspapers).

A quintuplet arrangement of circles, also from Cheesefoot Head. As with the previous photograph, hoaxing was ruled out as a possible cause for the circles (photo Southern Newspapers).

several occasions though, they have publicly conceded that an 'unknown intelligence' could well be at work and, in their book, cite several odd occurrences that have taken place in and around the circle formations.

In 1987, for instance, Colin Andrews met with a string of peculiar happenings during his examination of an oval ring located in a wheatfield at Kimpton, near Andover. Villagers had reported strange noises coming from the field prior to the appearance of the ring, and one teenage boy had witnessed an orange, glowing object in the vicinity.

Colin made regular trips to the field, and on the 29th June he was standing inside the ring when a black flash, as though the Sun had been blotted out, caused him to flinch momentarily. On looking up, he could see nothing to account for the temporary blackout, but admitted to feeling very uneasy about the incident. On the same day, his dog had shown a marked reluctance to approach the ring when taken into the field by Colin's father, and had become violently ill when it eventually stepped inside the circle.

On another occasion, in the same field, Colin was startled to hear a crackling noise similar to static electricity, coming from an unknown source about eight feet from where he was standing. The noise escalated to such a pitch that he fully expected an explosion to occur. The noise stopped abruptly - it had lasted no more than six seconds altogether.

Another team, Jenny Randles and Paul Fuller of BUFORA (British UFO Research Association) took a very down-to-earth look at the phenomenon, and enraged a large section of the 'E.T.' fraternity by refusing to endorse the alien landing hypothesis. Their aim was to conduct an unbiased investigation into the mystery, separating fact from myth wherever possible.

They looked closely at the hoax theory, favoured by many as the answer to the circles mystery. Numerous wild claims had been made to the media by self-confessed perpetrators of the phenomenon, all eager to show how easy it was to recreate the desired effect. They hadn't taken into account, however, the growing expertise of the small band of researchers whose pioneering studies had revealed several major circle characteristics that, to date, have proved impossible to fake in an artificial manner. The absence of physical damage to the cereal crops, for example, and the distinctive swirling , layering and banding of the flattened stems.

Paul Fuller, in a book he co-authored with Jenny Randles entitled *Controversy of the Circles*, examined the hoax theory in minute detail and came to the conclusion that, although some of the circles were undoubtedly hoaxes, the majority were definitely not the product of human ingenuity.

Another speculative theory by the BUFORA pair, that military RPVs (remotely piloted vehicles) may have been responsible for the circles, was quickly dismissed.

Details of these top-secret devices, known as 'Drones', are understandably not readily available to the public, yet the investigators claim knowledge of two factories in southern England that are responsible for the manufacture of these furturistic vehicles.

Believed to be small, silent, oddly-shaped craft capable of eluding radar detection, it was considered possible that they could have formed the circles during the course of experimental test flights and landings. Owing to the lack of hard data regarding R.P.V.s, an accurate assessment of their performance capabilities was out of the question, leaving the BUFORA team no other option than to mark it down as 'unproven speculation'.

UFOs; helicopters; parallel universes; ley lines; electro-magnetic forces - the list of theories seemed endless, but still the circles defied explanation - or did they?

Since the first publicised appearance of the circles in 1980, Dr Terence Meaden, Director of the Wiltshire-based Tornado and Storm Research Organisation, had been quietly, and methodically studying the phenomenon. His findings were to create a different kind of storm amongst the various research groups - a storm of controversy!

"I believe that atmospheric vortices, or whirlwinds, are responsible for the formation of the cropfield circles," he told an astonished public.

"Ridiculous!" came the vociferous reply of many, "How on earth could a whirlwind produce such a perfect pattern without causing significant damage to the surrounding crop?"

Whirlwinds, generally viewed as travelling spirals of destruction, are nothing new to this country. A surprising number of them form every year during the summer months, but Dr Meaden was proposing something different - a stationary whirlwind.

This type of vortex, well known to meteorologists, usually forms in the same manner as the more conventional whirlwind, but is prevented from moving laterally when obstructed by a sudden rise in the terrain (such as a hill). Dr Meaden claimed that any whirlwind subjected to this restriction would almost certainly

have a lifespan of only a few seconds which would explain the mysterious way in which the circles suddenly appeared, as if by magic, in the middle of an unmarked cropfield.

Improbable? Maybe, but this account of an incident that took place at Westbury in 1982 may provide a clue as to the exact nature of the phenomenon. The case is cited in Dr Meaden's very informative, and highly acclaimed book, *The Circles Effect and its Mysteries.*

DATELINE: SATURDAY 3RD JULY: APROXIMATLEY 6.00PM

The turbulence of an afternoon thunderstorm had long since abated, when local man, Mr R. Barnes, first noticed a strange disturbance in a nearby cropfield.

"My attention was first drawn to a 'wave' coming through the heads of the cereal crop in a straight line, at a constant speed," he wrote. Estimating that the "wave" was moving at about fifty miles an hour, he watched as the advancing 'line' crossed the field in a wide, shallow arc.

"The agency, though invisible, behaved like a solid object throughout," he informed Dr Meaden, "It showed no variation in speed, line, or strength."

The 'line' suddenly dropped, and swept a clean circle, seventy-five feet radius, in about four seconds! The agency, or whirlwind, then disappeared completely leaving Mr Barnes the only witness to its short-lived but spectacular, performance.

Fair enough, you may think. There's no denying that a whirlwind could have formed some of the single circles, but what about the evenly spaced triple sets. Surely even a stationary whirlwind could not be expected to hop about in such a precise manner.

Dr Meaden acknowleged at the time, that this was an unusual formation, but pointed out that it was not unheard of in meteorological circles(!) for stationary whirlwinds to form in triplets, with a central funnel, and two smaller 'satellite' funnels.

During the period 1980-1989, Dr Meaden has studied over six hundred circle formations at various locations. The ever-changing pattern of the mystery circles has led him to revise his theory accordingly, but he remains convinced that they are weather-related phenomenon created by a species of plasma vortex with properties similar to that of ball lightning.

This low energy vortex, he claims, is capable of forming in mid-air before, occasionally, descending to ground level. The mystery circles, he believes, are the result of those that happened to come down in cropfields.

The BUFORA research team, again incurring the wrath of a great many UFO devotees, found much to recommend in the vortex theory, and felt that this was the most plausible explanation to date. They joined forces with Dr Meaden's Tornado and Storm Research Organisation in 1987, to conduct a quantitative survey of the phenomenon. The detailed results of this survey can be found in *Controversy of the Circles*.

There are weaknesses too, in this theory, highlighted objectively in the BUFORA book, not least of which is the fact that it has yet to be accepted by established scientists.

Fellow meteorologists, likewise, are not all in agreement with Dr Meaden's findings. Dr Paul Mason, Head of Physical Research Section at the Metorological Office in Bracknell, for instance, wrote the following letter to Paul Fuller in February 1989...

"With regard to Dr Meaden's vortex theory, I am afraid that as far as the circles are concerned, I don't think it is at all relevant - all observations of such, and other, meteorological vortices, are highly turbulent and irregular. I just cannot conceive how any meteorological vortex could produce the highly ordered patterns seen in the cornfields. In summary, I do not support the meterological explanation at all. I am sure my views will delight ufologists, but in spite of difficulties, I think the most probable explanation is the ingenuity of some dedicated hoaxers.

Pat Delgado and Colin Andrews have also made it clear that they do not support the vortex theory. On the other hand, Dr John Snow, Associate Professor of Meteorology at Purdue University in America, does support the hypothesis that the circles are produced by some form of vortex resulting from air-flow over or around a terrain feature (hills, etc.). He is also of the opinion that the 'sensationalism' surrounding the circles mystery is hampering further serious scientific investigations.

The circles are now a well-established part of Hampshire folklore, and look set to grace our cropfields for many years to come. Years of investigation and research have so far failed to provide absolute proof of the agency involved in the circle formations. Can we expect to see Dr Terence Meaden's vortex theory win the day during the coming decades? Or will the controversy rage into the next century, unending, like the circles themselves?

Unlike the UFO problem, the question is not do they exist, but why. They appear, year after year, for all to see and for some to study, challenging our ability to unravel their secrets. Is there any possibility that the mystery will deepen? Could there be any one development that would stamp a giant question mark on years of research into the circles phenomenon?

The answer is yes.

They could stop appearing!

FILE 11
THE TRUTH IS 'HERE'

'Life on Mars' blazed the headlines on 7th August 1996, triggering a huge surge of renewed interest in the UFO phenomenon. Could we now expect official confirmation of alien intelligences or, at the very least, an explanation for the many hundreds of strange craft seen and reported in our skies with increasing regularity?

Sadly, the answer in no, not yet, but there are many in the field of UFO investigation who believe that a public announcement by the World's Governments, confirming the existence of extra-terrestrial intelligences, is imminent...

The examination of the Martian meteorite uncovered 'Strong circumstantial evidence of possible early Martian life' according to NASA scientists, a revelation that jolted the world with its implications.

"If there's evidence of life on Mars, no matter how small or how long ago, who's to say there isn't life elsewhere - not so small and not extinct?" I was asked during one of my interviews for this book.

"Nobody in their right mind," I was tempted to reply but, regretfully, I knew that if he delved too deeply he'd find more than one willing to support the 'We are alone' theory.

This theory however, is now so implausible and unacceptable to an enquiring public, that reports of UFO sightings are now being widely accepted as fact and not as the figment of someone's vivid imagination.

Sightings around the world are increasing daily and the UK is no exception. In 1995, a British Airways 737 crew reported a huge 'wedge-shaped' object pass down the starboard side of their aircraft at great speed. No sound could be heard and no turbulence felt, despite its close proximity. The object was lit with a number of small lights, clearly visible to the shaken crew as it shot past.

In Glastonbury, several sightings of a huge triangular UFO by very creditable witnesses has baffled experts. Massive in structure with pulsating lights that cast an eerie glow over the surrounding countryside, the amazing craft has been seen on over fifty occasions. One witness, asked if he thought the craft was extra-terrestrial, replied that it looked more like something that earth technology might create, "In say, two hundred years time!" Another witness felt that he was being monitored, "By a civilization from our own future."

Mysterious indeed, yet is the truth

still 'out there' as the *X Files* will have us believe or is it, in the words of one of my witnesses, "No, it's not out there - the truth is HERE!"

"We know from research that certain areas act as windows, allowing UFOs to visit. We believe, from the number of reports being received, that the south coasts acts as one of these windows."

These words, by Skysearch founder, Larry Dean, added a modern slant to the UFO mystery, allowing thousands upon thousands of computer orientated citizens to identify with the phenomenon. It also served to highlight a number of sightings in Hampshire that continue to bewilder the experts...

In the early hours of 18th August 1995, two Southampton taxi drivers were startled by the sudden appearance of a glowing UFO over the city's docks area. Mike McMahon and Mike Swatridge could only watch in awe as the object scorched across the sky at incredible speed,before veering off north towards Winchester.

"It was fantastic," said Mike McMahon, "I've never seen anything like it before. It was shifting so fast, it was unbelievable."

As the UFO changed direction, both men saw red and green lights inside the main body of the craft, an observation that would almost certainly rule out shooting stars (meteors) or any other form of natural phenomena. Reports of the same object later filtered through from Warsash (on the eastern outskirts of Southampton) where people were jolted from sleep by a loud rumbling noise as the object passed over, "Lighting up the sky like daylight."

"I particularly enjoyed the IFO (Identified Flying Objects) chapter," Paul Fuller (see Foreword) once told me, "It may make people think twice before they jump to conclusions about what they're seeing."

I agreed with Paul and, since the first edition of this book, something new has come along to invade our night skies...

"It was incredible," said one witness, "It was a massive circular object with bright coloured lights circling around it - it didn't make a sound."

"It moved slowly in a circular pattern with flickering beams of coloured light spinning around a central white light," claimed another.

The 'UFO' however, was also witnessed by thousands of others who were standing right underneath it at Ocean Village in Southampton. They had no trouble

An unidentified flying object photographed and well-authenticated on America. Similar objects have been seen over Hampshire and the Isle of Wight and may have been the cause of Mike McMahon's sighting.

at all in identifying the mystery lights - a fantastic laser light show that lit up the sky for miles around. Advance publicity it seemed, hadn't reached all the parts it should have!

Whilst I agreed with Paul that IFOs need to be brought to public attention, I also believe that 'over-kill' can be disadvantageous. It would be a great shame if a genuine UFO were to be ignored with a shrug of the shoulders and a muttered, "Branson again," (see File 3) dismissal...

Away from the cities, the picturesque countryside of Hampshire has also attracted its share of baffling encounters, not least the eerie experience shared by a family driving through the

Swanmore/Bishops Waltham area on a cold, starry night in October 1994.

It was around 9.30pm when the family first caught sight of a strange object flitting between the trees alongside their car.

"I thought it might have been an aeroplane at first," one of the boys explained, "but then I realised it was going too slow. There were two bright white lights underneath and four bars, like an electric fire, on top."

The UFO shadowed the car for several minutes before finally altering course and shooting off at high speed. A strange and frightening fog then appeared from nowhere and enveloped the car with suffocating tentacles of writhing mist. Until that moment the night had been clear and mist free.

When they eventually arrived home, none the worse for their amazing encounter, they were intrigued to hear that several sightings of a similar object had already been reported in the same area of countryside.

Elaborate hoaxes, mistaken identification or merely flights of fancy? Are we perhaps, looking too hard for proof that we aren't all alone in a big, dark universe? All the witnesses in this book, to the best of my knowledge, genuinely believe they've seen something extraordinary - beyond the sphere of earth technology. Without exception, every one of them impressed me enormously with their sincerity and honesty. Many of them believed that life elsewhere was far more probable than improbable. Others weren't so sure.

One brave young lady KNOWS there's life elsewhere - and often wishes there wasn't...!

THE SOUTHAMPTON CONTACT

Karen Smith was just seven years old when her stark, incredible story of alien visitation began to unfold. It started innocently enough, with Karen being woken up in the middle of the night by a blaze of light illuminating her bedroom.

Thinking it may have been an aeroplane, she went to the window to check, but nothing at all was visible in the night sky, Sleepily, she crawled back into bed and drifted off to sleep, determined to tell her mum in the morning of her nightime adventure.

"Mum told me she hadn't seen any lights," said Karen, "but when I went into the garden I found an egg-shaped indentation clearly marked in the frosty grass outside my bedroom window."

Recalling an odd incident from her early days, Karen remembers being told that she was playing with friends some time after this event when the talk came around to spacemen.

"Out of the blue, I just told them matter-of-factly that I'd seen spacemen and been taken away by them. They all started to laugh at me, thinking I was fibbing but when I burst into tears they realised that something strange was going on. Years later, when my story came out, one of the girls got in touch with me and told me that she'd always been bothered by what I'd said that day and felt, even then, that I'd been telling the truth."

Nightmares began to plague Karen's teenage years - recurring dreams in which she lay helplessly paralysed, terrified by her predicament and nauseated by the pungent odour of sulphur that seemed to be all around her. At this stage, she had no inkling of the incredible events that were about to test her faith and courage to the absolute limit.

"I was twenty one when I saw my 'visitors' for the first time," Karen revealed, "I've since realised that the major encounters occur every seven years, although I've been visited on several occasions between these gaps."

On the night in question, Karen was asleep in bed when a silent, blinding explosion of white light filled the bedroom with dazzling brilliance. Waking with a start of fright, she found at first that she appeared to be pinned to her bed by an unknown force, but slowly, she began to turn over - and came face-to-face with her first visitor.

"It was absolutely terrifying," Karen remembered, "there was this small, grey humanoid figure, only about four foot tall, stood right in front of me. It didn't appear to be clothed in any way, unless it was a very close fitting type of garment. The face was wide, with a very small mouth - more a hole than anything, the eyes were dark, slanted and very big."

Despite her fear Karen felt that she'd seen her visitor before, a feeling that came deep from her subconscious. It was then that she noticed other figures in the room.

"They were only about two feet tall, but really scary to look at," she said, "I believe they were like assistants to the 'greys' but I hated looking at them. There was a smell about them as well, a really strong smell of sulphur that was almost overpowering."

Karen then felt herself lifted from the bed without any visible means of support.

"At this point the high pitched humming noise I'd become aware of began to decrease in intensity and I began to feel a little more in control of the situation. The next thing I knew it was all over. I was back in bed, the room was empty, and I was bloody relieved about that, believe me!"

The next meeting, seven years later, was to prove even more traumatic...

"I was twenty eight by then," Karen said, "I'd gone to bed early one night and was again woken by this blinding light. I sat up quickly and saw several figures coming out of the light. It looked as though they were coming straight out of the bedroom wall, as though they were being transported by the light beam itself."

Again she found herself held motionless by an invisible power, unable even to scream out to her husband downstairs. This time however, Karen remained conscious of her surroundings and became slowly aware that she was about to undergo an examination.

"They inserted this glowing tube into my abdomen," she said calmly. "It didn't hurt in any way but I did feel this burning sensation that led down to my ovarian area. I don't know what the purpose of the examination was, but I believe they were withdrawing eggs from my body for some reason."

The examination was over quickly and Karen felt a cold instrument placed against her forehead. This appeared to be some form of anaesthetic,for she immediately began to feel drowsy and fell into a deep sleep. When she awoke, her visitors had gone.

During the time I spent interviewing Karen, I asked several questions that I thought may prove the story a hoax - a carefully orchestrated story to attract business for the tattoo parlour she runs with her partner, Richard, in Southampton.

The parlour (now called 'Alien Tattoos') needed no such publicity. Business has always been brisk and the added publicity seems to have attracted more journalists than customers. When I suggested to Karen that some cynics may look to this as a publicity stunt, she shrugged her shoulders with a resignation born of many such accusations.

"I never wanted this story to come out at all," she told me wearily. "If I hadn't agreed to talk to one particular investigator about my experiences, it never would have come to light."

In a world now buzzing with startling revelations about the UFO enigma however, this was a major scoop and it wasn't long before Karen was besieged with reporters, all eager to hear her story. She met their media hype with stoicism and patience, told her story simply and without embellishment, cringed at some of the wild inaccuracies printed for sensationalism, and then attempted to regain some form of normality.

"I've no reason to lie," she told me in explanation, "I'm telling you, quite simply, of my experiences. If you believe me, that's okay, but if you don't then that's okay too!"

I agreed that this was a very good philosophy and became totally absorbed during the rest of the interview. I can remember quite clearly, about half way through the session, feeling suddenly shocked by what I was hearing. The moment that sealed my belief in Karen's story however, came when I asked her what she thought of her visitors and their intentions. For the first time, her voice took on a hard edge of anger.

"I think they're arrogant little bastards," she said with feeling. "I

Karen Smith the Hampshire girl whose close encounters with aliens led to intense military activity. Here she poses with a likeness of one of her 'visitors' - four-foot alien creatures who have contacted her every seven years since childhood.

think they've been given this job to do and they intend doing it with or without my permission."

I'd expected some rosy explanation and homespun philosophy about our role in the universe. Instead, this totally unrehearsed and completely natural reaction left me with the uneasy feeling that we definitely aren't alone and haven't been for some considerable time...

When asked if the seven-year interval between major encounters had any bearing on the time it took to travel from wherever they came from, Karen shook her head slowly. "No, I know they're not from this planet but I believe that they're actually based here. The seven year gap, I'm positive, has more to do with the fact that the human body's cells regenerate completely every seven years or so. I'd guess that's about as good a way as any for them to study us."

"Have you ever tried to resist in any way?" I asked, "and how do they react if you show aggression?"

Answering quickly, Karen allowed a trace of grim satisfaction to edge her reply:

"Yes, I'm finding that I can cope with them a lot better now than when I was younger. I get the distinct impression that they're afraid of human aggression and always tend to pull back a little out of harm's way when it's directed at them. They seem to realise when they've perhaps gone too far and withdraw quickly."

What of the 'greys?', does she now recognize any of them and is there any one in particular she relates to?

"One of them, a female, tries to make more of an effort to reassure me that they mean no harm."

Anticipating my obvious next question, Karen said, "Don't' ask me how I know it's female - feminine intuition I suppose you could call it."

Karen lives in a secluded area of Hampshire, on a smallholding set in approximatley fifteen acres of land. Since her story came to light, a different kind of aerial harassment has added to her problems - helicopters.

"We were suddenly plagued by low flying helicopters at all hours of the day and night," she said. "I could see them filming the area directly around the house. I got so fed up in the end that I phoned the Ministry of Defence to ask why they were doing it. They told me it was just everyday military manoeuvres, but I'm certain it's more than that."

Karen's incredible account of one human being's encounters with alien intelligences makes astounding reading and may prove too disturbing or unbelievable for many to accept. Karen would be the first to agree - it wouldn't be the first time she's come up against a wall of disbelief, even though she's volunteered to be hypnotically regressed to reveal the truth.

For my own part I'd gone into the interview warily, not knowing quite what to expect. At the very least I think I expected to be talking to a slightly eccentric lady with a flair for publicity.

Instead I found myself talking to an ordinary Hampshire girl who showed not one iota of eccentricity throughout the whole interview. It was a remarkable experience to find myself listening to this harrowing story and realising, with a little jolt of awareness, that I believed every word she was telling me!

At one stage of the questioning Karen told me that she was certain her visitors didn't want attention drawn to them in any way. I pointed out that she wasn't exactly being discreet by talking to me and certainly wasn't looking to win any favours by using them as publicity material for her business. Karen's reply was defiant - a very human reaction to aggression from any quarter.

"They've exploited me without permission," she told me forcibly. "Now it's my turn to damn well exploit them for a change."

VIEWPOINT

Once again, it's time to reveal my own views on the UFO mystery. Well, it hasn't changed a lot since the book was first published but I'm now absolutely positive that events relating to the phenomena are escalating so rapidly in the world that a shattering revelation regarding UFOs is imminent.

The release of the controversial 'Roswell footage', for instance, showing the autopsy on a humanoid figure recovered from a crashed UFO in Mexico in 1947, raised a huge argument for and against its authenticity, but far more subtle reasons have been suggested for its release. Hampshire's own crop circle expert, Colin Andrews, uncovered a remarkable story whilst lecturing in Los Angeles.

Along with top Japanese government official, Johsen Takano, he'd been invited to a showing of the Roswell autopsy film supposedly released by a retired military cameraman named Santilli.

After the show, Colin had asked Mr Takano what he'd thought about the film and was astounded when the Japanese official told him he'd seen it a year previously, courtesy of the US Government.

Real or fake, the undisputed fact of this story is that the film was released with the blessing of the US Government.

Why? Was it a deliberate attempt to cast doubt about the whole Roswell incident which, to this day, is still subject to massive controversy, or was it, as Colin suggests, an attempt to gauge public opinion regarding the presence of extra-terrestrials.

If the latter is correct, can it be that they're thinking of releasing even more authentic proof regarding UFOs and their occupants in the near future?

If further proof were needed regarding the reality of UFOs, I don't think we need look further than Nick Pope who, for three years was top UFO investigator for the Ministry of Defence.

During his time running the Air Secretariat's UFO desk he became fully convinced of the reality of UFOs.

"Almost five per cent of all reported sightings were officially classified 'Unknown'", he revealed. "I believe these five per cent were probably of extra-terrestrial origin...!"

The long, patient wait for enlightenment may soon be over. The old century is drawing to a close, with a bright new beginning beckoning in the year 2000. If all the evidence is correct, historians will mark the twenty-first century as the time the UFO mystery was finally solved and the human race discovered it was not alone...

ACKNOWLEDGEMENTS

It would be impossible to mention individually all the people who have helped in the completion of this book. For anyone omitted I can only apologise and assure them of my heartfelt gratitude for their efforts.

Special mention goes to my wife, Susan, and our children Andrew and Sarah who gave up so much of their leisure time to enable me to complete the original work - and saw it through to this new and revised edition. Thanks also to David (for spreading the word) and to Steve Gerrard for his able assistance. Special thanks to Paul Fuller for his expertise and constructive criticism - and for agreeing to write the Foreword. Finally a big thank you to Clive Brooks, without whom nothing would have been possible.